10-6-58.

TV
and SCREEN WRITING

Compiled and edited by Lola Goelet Yoakem

Introduction by Hugh Gray

ERIK BARNOUW

GOMER COOL

REUVEN FRANK

FRANK GRUBER

LOIS JACOBY

HAL KANTER

JESSE L. LASKY, JR.

STEPHEN LONGSTREET

MARY C. MCCALL, JR.

FRANK S. NUGENT

CHARLES PALMER

IVAN TORS

EUGENE VALE

MALVIN WALD

ELIHU WINER

LOLA GOELET YOAKEM

TV AND SCREEN WRITING

University of California Press
Berkeley & Los Angeles
1958

University of California Press
Berkeley and Los Angeles

Cambridge University Press
London, England

© 1958 by The Regents of the University of California

Library of Congress Catalog Card Number: 58-8654
Printed in the United States of America

Designed by Ward Ritchie

Foreword   1046741

Seventeen successful working writers in films, television, and radio have written this volume. Their purpose is to share with the new writer their experience and special knowledge, not merely of the media in which they write but also of the intricate professional world that today's mass-media writer inhabits: a world of the major studios, independent producers, networks, advertising agencies, syndicates, sponsors, investors, censors, agents, pressure groups, foundations, government agencies—and, last but not least, guilds.

The Writers Guild of America is the national organization of writers in radio, screen, and television. Lola G. Yoakem headed the WGA committee that organized this book.* The very existence of such a book as this is indicative of the WGA attitude toward the new writer. The Guild has tried to help him in many ways: it has prided itself on the low WGA initiation fee, and it has made research studies and conducted clinics on writers' markets and professional problems. But perhaps the most important boon to the new writer now entering television, radio, or films is the fact that WGA, building upon the work of earlier guilds, has achieved a group of significant collective-bargaining agreements. Many of the authors of this book remember times when the writer

---

* In 1955 a subcommittee of active Writers Guild members (west) met to discuss the idea of a book of actual working experiences of professionals in TV and screen writing. That original committee included James Warner Bellah, Robert Carson, Stephen Longstreet, Mary C. McCall, Jr., Eugene Vale, and Lola G. Yoakem as chairman. The group was a part of the WGAw Public Relations Committee, then headed by Allen Rivkin and later by Frank S. Nugent. Because of the scope of the work and length of time required for preparatory coördination, the subcommittee did not meet after 1955, but the book project was continued and concluded by Lola Yoakem as a member of the Public Relations Committee.

in films or broadcasting received little money and no credits and had to sell his work outright to get anything. These writers are glad that they can welcome the new writers to a better state of affairs even though the writing profession is still confronted with many unsolved problems.

The Writers Guild of America is grateful to the authors of this book for assigning all royalties to a special WGA educational fund.

ERIK BARNOUW
National Chairman
Writers Guild of America

A Word About the Writers Guild of America

Writing is lonely work. Because of this fact, writers are naturally not inclined either to form or to join organizations. However, professional writers learned through experience that they needed protection of their rights and literary property and security in equitable working conditions and compensation, and that these could best be achieved through the strength of common determination. Thus the Writers Guild of America came into being.

Before a writer can become a member of the Guild, he must either have commercially disposed of material rights or have become a staff or contract writer in television, radio, or motion pictures. His subsequent status as a Guild member depends upon his continuing credits on a free-lance or contractual basis. Guild membership guarantees protections of rights and minimum compensation, but it is not a substitute for talent—professional ability alone must secure employment for the writer.

The Guild prevents exploitation of talent. It demands for its members adequate and fair recognition as creators of literary material used for television, radio, and motion pictures; it protects subsidiary rights, and assists in securing payment for reuse of filmed scripts; it makes certain that writing credits are given fairly and responsibly.

EDMUND HARTMANN
President, Writers Guild of America, west

HALSTED WELLS
President, Writers Guild of America, east

Contents

INTRODUCTION   1
                        Hugh Gray

IDEA TO FINAL FORM   7
                        Eugene Vale

NOVEL TO SCREENPLAY   14
                        Stephen Longstreet

THE OPENING SCENES   20
                        Frank S. Nugent

TV—LIVE OR FILM?   25
                        Elihu Winer

RELIGIOUS AND BIBLICAL FILMS   34
                        Jesse L. Lasky, Jr.

THE WESTERN   39
                        Frank Gruber

COMEDY   45
                        Hal Kanter

SCIENCE FICTION   54
                        Ivan Tors

FACTUAL TV   59
                        Reuven Frank

BUSINESS FILM   66
                        Charles Palmer

THE BESPOKE SCRIPT   83
                        Mary C. McCall, Jr.

RADIO   87
                        Gomer Cool

Contents

WRITING CONTESTS   94
    Erik Barnouw

THE BUSINESS OF WRITING   99
    Lola Goelet Yoakem

THE HOLLYWOOD MARKET   107
    Malvin Wald

THE NEW YORK MARKET   112
    Lois Jacoby

ABBREVIATIONS   119

GLOSSARY   121

Introduction

As a general rule, the aspiring screen and television writer
has no way of establishing contact with the professional
world. Outside the few colleges where creative dramatic
writing is part of the curriculum, the beginning writer has
until now had few opportunities to learn at first hand from
contemporary working writers the answers to problems that
confront him.

Here, at last, is an answer: a book of practical advice based
on actual experience in the fields of screen and television by
writers actively engaged in these fields. Each contributor
poses a common problem and offers a personal solution. In
addition, certain informative articles may hold a pertinent
value for established writers as well as for the newcomers
and students.

All the valuable advice in the present book will not avail
the aspiring writer anything unless he realizes what the term
"writer" means in the full context of the dramatic arts as
they are practiced: the particular kind of creative person
whose image and function emerge clearly from the body of
this book. His concern is with the turning of narrative into
drama, from the Bible to interplanetary fiction; with action,

both physical and dramatic; with the task of understanding the public as audience; with the preparation of material to meet the specific needs of programs and of personalities; and with a dozen other secrets of the trade.

As the following pages clearly reaffirm, then, a dramatist is not primarily a man of letters—he is a man of actions. Fine descriptive writing, elaborate imagery, and the narrative prose-poem are not his tools. These exist to provide the reader of words with a mental substitute, a counterpart, for what is present, in flesh and blood and action, to the audience in the theater or in images on the motion-picture or television screen.

Indeed, the first great creative artists of silent motion pictures welcomed the new medium as an escape from what Eisenstein called the tyranny of the literary playwright. D. W. Griffith, a frustrated writer who secretly dreamed of being the Shakespeare of the American legitimate theater and who at first despised motion pictures, used no scripts. For *The Birth of a Nation,* the novel *The Clansman* was his guide. *Intolerance,* on the other hand, was his own original idea. Here, however, even the inspirational genius of Griffith, the great improviser, in dealing with so vast, so complex, and as it happened so confused a concept, would have been well served by a screen writer. The world might then have possessed a true film masterpiece instead of an immortal failure. No example could better serve to illustrate the basic function of the dramatic writer. *Intolerance* failed, as many other motion pictures have since failed, because it lacked true balance of form and clarity of concept. Griffith, profusely imaginative and therefore not readily amenable to the discipline of artistic economy, was experimenting with a new medium that, of its nature, tends to diffusion and distraction and is forever challenging the constraint of structure. In other words, the architecture of *Intolerance* was bad. From the inception it needed a dramatic architect—as good a definition as any of the stage, screen, or television writer. He

2

is an architect whose material is action, and who plots the interplay of the stress, strain, and pull of conflicting natural forces in men and women. The improvisations of Griffith were a concomitant of his pioneering preoccupation with the new tools of drama: the camera and the film editor's scissors. With these tools the film editor, almost more than anyone else, helped create the art of motion pictures. But even so, a writer at his elbow gave him his sense of character drawing and even the rhythm of his editing: namely the Victorian novelist in general, and Dickens especially. The tyranny of the playwright against which Eisenstein, an equally ardent admirer of Dickens, revolted was the tyranny in the theater of the word for the word's sake. Like Griffith, Eisenstein too was looking for a new form of dramatic structure suitable to a visual medium, and so for a new form of playwriting.

One of the more articulate, though not always one of the more lucid, of the philosophizing practitioners of the art of motion pictures, Eisenstein described the architectural function of the screen dramatist in what might seem an unexpected context. In the chapter of his book *Film Form* devoted to the structure of the film, he says of his now classic *Potemkin:*

Potemkin looks like a chronicle (or newsreel) of an event but it functions as a drama.

The secret of this lies in the fact that the chronicle pace of the event is pitted to a severely tragic composition. And furthermore to tragic composition in its most canonic form; the five act tragedy. Events, regarded as almost naked facts, are broken into five tragic acts, being selected and arranged in sequence so that they answer the demands set by classical tragedy; a third act quite distinct from the second, a fifth distinct from the first and so on.

The choice of a five act structure in particular for this tragedy was, of course, by no means accidental, but was the result of prolonged natural selection—but we need not go into this history here. Enough that for the basis of our drama we took a structure that had been particularly tested by the centuries.

The dramatic architect works with rules as old as human nature itself. These rules may all be summed up in the simple statement: "If you start something, finish it!" The overtones, being concerned not with the dramatist but with his audience, are not moral but psychological. They express something basic to the way we all function, to our constituent needs. All must come to some kind of a conclusion. According to Aristotle, the action of a drama must necessarily have a beginning, a middle, and an end. This is ultimately true even of works that seem to set out to give it the lie or, at least, to ignore it, such as Cocteau's film *Le Sang d'un poète*. The greater the artist, the truer this will be. The essential fact remains, then, that the dramatist is the maker of plots with a pattern to fit certain specific requirements; patterns of shadow and sound

> And so not built at all
> And therefore built forever.

This structural planning may give the dramatist great satisfaction, but neither the satisfaction nor the work itself is complete until it has reached its audience. Here is the dramatists' major area of difficulty. The principal function of this book is to come to the rescue of the inexperienced writer in this very area.

An audience is a collection of widely differing individual tastes, some good, some bad; of likes and dislikes, mostly without rhyme or reason; of environmental prejudices and loyalties. Motion pictures and television cannot survive in their present form as public entertainment without the widest possible audience. Therefore, the screen and television writer, if he hopes to live by his profession, must plan according to a universally common denominator. He must face the realities of the commercial history of all entertainment, multiplied a millionfold in screen and television. The former was already on its way to becoming an industry from its inauguration as a peepshow. The latter has been a form of big business from its beginning. As early as 1914 it was estimated by the Italian paper *La Tribuna* that the film industry represented a capital investment of twelve billion francs and had thus risen to third rank in importance in international trade, next to wheat and coal. Today the billions involved are reckoned in dollars not francs.

These are the facts, and the young aspiring writer is frequently and not unjustifiably troubled by them. This is particularly true of the college student or, at least, of what used to be called the "reading man." A prolonged acquaintance with the humanities, at once the unique repository and salvation of our Western civilization, has engendered in him a devotion to certain ideals and artistic standards that, as he watches the motion-picture and television screen, he feels he must inevitably betray if he is to live by professional writing. In point of fact, most writers are not called upon to compromise. They write as well as they can, and if they are capable of great things they will carry their audiences with them—eventually.

It is likewise important for the young idealist, about to bestow himself upon the arts, to remember their history. At its very inception drama, although not commercial in today's sense, was not exactly a disinterested art. It was born, as Gilbert Murray has pointed out, from man's anxiety about the next year's harvest, and developed out of the magic by which man hoped to secure bountiful crops. Drama was the answer to the perennial threat of famine, when the great fear of mankind was scarcity. Although we have not entirely abandoned jujuism in all areas, it is no longer thought to be the only way to ensure our survival. Indeed scarcity is not the problem of the industrial age. The question today is not "Will there be any bread on the table?" but "What brand will it be?" In a world of such superabundance, advertising has replaced magic as a means of ensuring prosperity. So, with the tendency of drama to be related to survival, the quintessential dramatic form of the industrial age—television—has become an advertising medium.

5

Much as the young artist may deplore this, he should at the same time remember that the commercial is as old as Greek drama. The Athenian dramatist always wrote with his eye on the equivalent of an Oscar; the author of the old comedy appealed directly to the audiences for their support in this contest. There was a special moment set aside for this appeal, during which the chorus addressed the audience on behalf of the author, in words carefully prepared by the author himself. The balance is of course somewhat restored when we remember the brand of the merchandise. The problem of the audience, then, has been a perennial one, and many of the great dramatists have discussed it frankly. To the writer looking for rules of comedy, Farquhar, the Restoration author of a number of highly successful comedies, answers: "The rules of English comedy don't lie in the compass of Aristotle or his followers, but in the pit, box and galleries." Goethe's advice is: "Something for everyone. Only by mass you touch the mass." Nor, in our own time, is the challengingly original Jean Cocteau at variance with these two. Although he deplores the commercial conditions of the cinema that prevents its becoming what he believes it should be—the "supreme weapon of the poet"—he has no illusions about the target of the dramatist.

> Racine, Corneille, Molière, wrote for the boulevard of the period. And make no mistake about it; the boulevard means the ordinary public and it is to the ordinary public that the theater must appeal.

This is what the professional writer of plays for screen, television, and radio must do—he must appeal to the ordinary public. The following pages will help him do just that.

EUGENE VALE

Idea to Final Form

A writer is frequently asked about the basic ideas from which
he develops his stories and scripts. The original concept seems
to arouse as much interest as its subsequent growth. Often
almost magic powers are attributed to the truly creative
notion, as distinguished from one that is unproductive; indeed, it is often assumed that the "good" idea appears full-
blown in the writer's mind, replete with the capacity to grow
of itself along inherent and foreordained lines.

Nothing could be further from the truth. Any writer looking back upon his completed works will recall that the first
ideas have come to him in a rudimentary or fragmentary
form, in a variety of ways, and—more often than not—in a
completely unpredictable manner. Even the most disciplined
creator cannot control or willfully produce the moment of
inspiration, although he may have otherwise trained his
imaginative powers to be at their peak during certain working hours, or in a given set of circumstances, or under the
prodding of habit and idiosyncrasy. Further, at the instant
of their first appearance, some of his best ideas may have
gone almost unnoticed; only in retrospect can he recognize
which seed fell on fertile ground, which spark could be fanned

7

to creative flames, which notion was productive of results, fulfilling an earlier, uncertain promise.

Since the fundamental concept determines the outcome of the whole, it is of the utmost importance for the writer to choose wisely among many possible ideas before committing himself to the time and effort involved in full development. Yet, in the beginning, when he must make this selection, he has insufficient material upon which to base his choice.

Being incomplete, the initial notion cannot yet be "good"; indeed, many a promising idea may have been squashed, or rejected by an outsider, because it was offered too soon, submitted to impersonal view before its potential had been given a chance to manifest itself.

The very nature of the primary impulse is such as to elude definition. It is not identical with the subject matter, though this may be part of it; nor with the theme, though this may be found in it. It may be a childhood memory, a dominant character trait, even a glimpse of landscape or a fragment of dialogue.

The teeming brain never ceases to produce images, thoughts, ideas. Of these many are so fleeting as to escape the writer's attention almost entirely; some are briefly examined and rejected; others are considered, perhaps tested and worked on for a while, but ultimately forgotten. And then there are those which, for some reason or another, have a unique effect upon the writer and are not to be dismissed, no matter how hard he may try; they sometimes return to him over a period of years.

In its embryonic stage the ultimately successful idea seems to offer no other criterion than this intuitive affinity the writer feels for it. It has the peculiar capacity to stir his imagination and to remain in his memory until he has given it form.

Nor is it surprising that the initial selection should be made on this very personal basis. If a character, a situation, or a background has the power to affect the writer in some way, to linger on or to return to him over a period of time, it indicates some special, perhaps unconscious, appeal or meaning to him. In the arduous labors of developing the script, all the writer's creative energies are then likely to participate; he has his "heart in it," he is more than rationally interested, he takes pleasure in giving it form.

It stands to reason, therefore, that the subjective, rather than the objective, choice of the basic idea is likely to lead to the best results. Since no objectively valid value standards can be applied in the rudimentary stage, the writer's individual involvement is likely to prove the decisive factor.

Thus the original concept represents the most personal contribution of the writer. At the other end of the creative process is the final script, directed at a mass audience; to be understood, the personal must be cast into objective language—the subjective into a universally valid form.

It may be said, therefore, that the creative process begins in the subjective and ends in the impersonal. Individual emotion must be expressed in terms of the commonly identifiable experience. Only in this manner can the dramatist achieve the desired effect of evoking in the individual spectator the emotions he intended to stir. The poet can largely dispense with this detour, aiming directly at the heart of his reader. But the television-script writer must follow the full span from the subjective to the objective in order to reproduce in the individual spectator the subjective response once again.

In developing his basic idea toward this goal, the writer discovers that the final form makes its demands upon the earliest stages of growth. On one hand, the primary concept remains the seed around which the crystal conglomerates; it continues to be the mainspring that powers the story and script. On the other hand, the writer must soon ask himself which direction to take in order to reach the objective of the particular form he has selected, if indeed the fundamental idea lends itself to that objective.

Surprises are not infrequent in the course of working out the preconceived plan. The idea that had seemed so right

9

for a half-hour show really requires an hour, or perhaps even ninety minutes, for full development. Conversely, the strong situation that had promised to provide all the conflict and drama for a feature film reveals itself as too introverted a character study in its final resolution.

As the various outlets for the writer's creative efforts change in nature, it becomes increasingly important for him to learn how to evaluate the potential of his idea at the earliest possible stage.

In the past, it was not unusual for the same writer to be equally proficient in the fields of poetry, short story, novel, and drama. Although the boundaries have never been drawn too sharply, the degree of specialization seems to have been influenced by the spirit of the times; by the individual talent of the writer determining his predilection for the epic or the dramatic, for the short story or the novel, for comedy or tragedy; and, finally, by the technical innovations at the disposal of the creator, which, at different times, have also changed the living patterns of his audience.

We are now in another period of flux in which boundaries melt and specialization becomes diminished. During the past few decades the trend was toward a rather definite classification of writers as novelists or magazine writers, as radio or screen writers, as TV writers or playwrights, with further subdivisions in each field. But the upheavals brought about by the advent of television have not yet run their course; the rapid transformations taking place in all the outlets open to creative talent are dissolving each new classification almost as soon as it is established. The former New York television writer and his Hollywood colleague may now be working side by side on half-hour Westerns; the magazine writer has sold some hour dramas; and many screen writers are dividing their time between movies, the stage, novels, and television.

By necessity, if not by choice, more and more writers are becoming experts in different forms. Consequently a writer no longer has to reject an idea because it happens to be unsuitable to the specific medium in which he is working at that moment. Instead, he can jot it down, file it away for future reference, and take it out again when it has either ripened to the point where he feels impelled to work it out or when it can fulfill the demands of an outside request.

Since the creative mind produces ideas spontaneously and without much regard for the length of stories required by a certain magazine or the running time of a particular television series, the writer cannot promptly coax, prod, or force his mind to deliver what he needs at any given time. He can, however, train himself to recognize in the flow of ideas their hidden or potential merit, and thus to build up a backlog that becomes not only the storehouse but the fundamental wealth of any writer.

At what point, from what part, and in what manner, he draws from this storehouse, depends upon so many variable and individual factors that no general rules can be drawn. Inner or outer impulses beyond the writer's control may play the decisive role; all he can consciously and willfully do may be to match the right idea to the desired objective.

The interplay between the creative impulse and the strictures of the form poses some of the most fascinating problems confronting the writer. At times, particularly while struggling with some of the harsher restrictions imposed by the television medium, it may be well for the writer to remember that completely unfettered creation is impossible and has never existed; that the mind, in order to escape chaos, has always sought form in spite of, or because of, its strictures. A writer cannot express an abstract thought without fitting it into an orderly sentence structure and submitting it to the rules of syntax. Throughout the centuries even the poets have vacillated between the extremes of the sonnet and free verse, between voluntarily imposing upon themselves the strict forms of regulated rhythm and rhyme and then, at other times, seeking to escape their confining rules.

Ideally, the writer who can afford to disregard all economic considerations would obey only his creative impulse;

overcome and compelled by an idea, he would decide which form would best lend itself to fulfill its inherent potential—novel, stage, screen, television. In practice, however, a majority of writers must give serious, if not foremost, consideration to the outlets for their work. If an idea chances to match the demand to perfection, the writer can proceed without difficulty. At the other end of the scale is the need to produce ideas exclusively to request, without any regard for the creative impulse.

In this interaction between the creative impulse and the demands of the form, the latter seems to play the decisive and determining role. For one thing, its theoretical needs are quite clearly established, derived, and conditioned by its very nature; they can neither be circumvented nor changed —they must be obeyed.

In a practical sense, the producer, editor, or publisher can be equally definite in his demands. He may request a story for a certain star, a script for a specific format, a novelette aimed primarily at the woman reader. He prescribes the length, he knows the budget and, not infrequently, the preferences of his star or sponsor.

Opposed to this, the creative impulse seems vague, groping, indecisive at times, and uncontrollable at others. A basic idea, still unformed, seems malleable enough to be guided in any desired direction. There seems no reason why the story material cannot be developed to suit either the necessary length or any other demand. It soon becomes apparent, however, that the basic story material has its inherent projections that are at least as stubborn as, and often even more incontrovertible than, the fixed demands of form and assignment. Anyone who has ever struggled with certain given story elements knows how deceptively pliable they may seem at first and yet how iron-willed they actually are. At some stage of development the flaws or inconsistencies are bound to come to the fore; the closer the final script, the less adequately can they be concealed or patched.

In the course of his creative labors, therefore, the writer

must look forward to his goal and go back to his basic ingredients; he must be aware of the demands the final form he has selected will impose on him, and he must examine the projections of the elements with which he is working. Only by a perfect blending of the two will he achieve the dynamic progression characteristic of the successful story and script.

The creative process, from the inception of an idea to the final form, is a striving for total awareness. Along the way, the writer is hindered by a lack of foreknowledge of the future and hampered by an insufficient awareness of the meaning of past decisions.

Only the completed work can give the full view, the full realization of intent and result, the full consciousness of idea and form—and that joyous moment of liberation known only to the creative mind as one of its singular rewards.

Novel to Screenplay

Motion pictures have created some fine craftsmen as well
as some remarkably good original authors. But the talents
that can produce lasting classics in literature must demand
a great deal more freedom than is afforded in a motion picture, even including the three-hour epic. The time element
is first and always the prime consideration when a screen
writer begins his task of adapting a novel into an acceptable
form for a motion picture.

Producers buy popular novels that have become best sellers
or at least have shown some promise of public acceptance.
This material is already tested, and therefore stands a better
chance of having a ready-made audience for the motion-
picture version. A book dealing with simple human problems
and their solutions usually makes a good motion picture;
great books and great literature do not. The authors of great
classics may probe into the hidden motives of human beings,
describing in splendid detail the innermost feelings and reactions of characters, so that the reader's imagination can
create the picture for him. Feelings defy pictorial treatment
in the modern movies, and—except for an occasional effort
like *War and Peace*—the classics are usually left alone.

14

A motion picture is a commercial product. The story may be a family saga, and cover several generations; it may move over the entire world; it may be written in several different styles to show the flavor of changing times, other countries, or contrasting speech. On the other hand, the story may not move beyond one town, one house, or even one room. However, one thing is certain: the main theme must be acceptable to the mass of ticket buyers, and be presented to them in a form they can easily comprehend and enjoy.

A novel bought for the screen may run to 600 pages and may contain as many as a hundred important characters. To begin, the writer must decide if he will try to do the entire book (*Gone with the Wind*), use only a small section (*East of Eden*), use only the title (*Life Begins at Forty*) and write an original story, or take something as well known as *The Front Page* and hide the fact by calling the movie *His Girl Friday*.

The dialogue in a novel is seldom usable in a screen-play; dialogue for the screen is an art, and can give the flavor of the book without quoting literatim. Even the dialogue of Hemingway or Faulkner cannot be used in its original form, but must be adapted by a screen writer. Screen dialogue must be succinct; a speech is of course permitted from time to time, but the dialogue *must* carry the story. Novels may have long chapters in which a single event is described at length in great detail; few screen shots last more than two or three minutes. A motion picture is a pasting together of tiny lengths of film, in which each individual shot must have style and pattern. Nothing is as dull as two persons simply talking. Even witty conversation becomes dull. The screen writer must use devices and small bits of "business" that the novelist never suggested. The use of the cigarette and the telephone is too easy; head scratching and hair arranging quickly become silly—the competent screen writer is faced in every line of dialogue by the problem of making the screen move.

Characters on the screen cannot talk like normal human

beings. "Damn," "hell," "lousy," "nuts," for example, cannot be used to express normal emotional reactions. Good scripts must bring life to a medium with many taboos.

The successful writer must achieve the flavor and mood of a 500-page novel in a 100-page screenplay.

Extended periods of time are difficult to accommodate on the screen. If a novel tells a story lasting ten or twenty years, it is best to make the major action of the screenplay occur in five or six years. Flashback is no longer popular; a skilled writer can achieve the same results in dialogue. Most screen actors are special types—more personalities than actors in the stage sense—and so it is best to adapt a character to acting standards in Hollywood. A story for the screen should include only scenes that can be played by the average Hollywood personality—a writer is judged, not by his screenplay, but by the finished picture.

Characters should be presented as fresh, exciting people, living in their time and place in society or as outcasts from society. They must first be shown doing something that will interest the audience. Formula dulls a character, and types should be avoided. The writer must face the problem of rules, codes, and ideas that have become part of picture making; dazzling effects in character are difficult to present.

A story is usually told by presenting a problem, or a series of problems, showing how the characters react to them, fight them, twist them, become trapped in them, and eventually free themselves. There is a climax, like a second-act curtain (but not to be confused with it), and a long "slide" for the end of the picture; with problem solved, the characters come together to live, love, or die. Few novels are written in this pattern; the main problem of the screen writer is to find this pattern and to bring it into his material.

Certain legends about the motion picture are, unfortunately, still in force. One is that the viewer must identify himself with a character in the film—must become part of the motion picture and see himself in the action. This legend has been made a basic rule, against which most screenplays are judged. Actually this approach is not true of all drama, or of all storytelling, yet the screen writer must work at least along the fringe of this idea. Another fixed ritual is that the average motion-picture viewer is not too intelligent and must not be given ideas that will tax his ability to understand. Many motion pictures are both adult and successful, but only an alert screen writer can get certain adult ideas into a script and have them kept there.

When I wrote the novel *Stallion Road*, I had no idea of making a film of it. When Warner Brothers bought it and asked me to write the screenplay, I was immediately confronted with many problems that, ironically enough, had really been of my own making. The novel covered a long period of time; it had about fifty major characters; its settings were many; it included long prose passages that could not be made pictorial.

As a screen writer, I had to present the world of the modern horse breeder within the budget of a million dollars. First, I cut the time span down to one season on the range. I then adapted the story to include only eight major characters. I streamlined the action and telescoped time and place to achieve a faster pace than in the novel.

The dialogue was a problem from the start. The characters usually talk at great length, but in pictures they must come to the point more quickly. Film dialogue must have pace and must not repeat any visual action. Screen characters do little meditative thinking, but become part of the action.

Only about 70 per cent of my screenplay ultimately became film footage. Many scenes that read well did not film well; cuts were made, action speeded up, speeches trimmed. I learned from this experience that it is better to overwrite a screenplay and then cut it, rather than to have to pad later.

Every story has a symbol. That of *Stallion Road* was, of course, the horse; so nearly every scene had a horse, saddle, a trophy, even a photograph—anything to carry the mood. I added violence to the screenplay because it helped to transmit the mood of the novel. In the novel, emotions were

17

often indicated in exposition; on the screen, these feelings were shown in action with fists, screaming voices, contorted faces.

Certain changes had to be made to fit studio casting requirements: for example, the little boy in the novel became a little girl in the screenplay, because the studio had a little girl under contract.

In order to solve the problem of time span, I used the voice of the main lead to carry the action over fast-moving montages to keep the story going and to avoid playing all the interlocking scenes of the plot.

I also wrote the screenplay for *Duel in the Sun* for David Selznick. This picture had a budget of several millions, and the problem was to make the story of the novel seem bigger than it was. Small events were exaggerated: scenes calling for only a few people were re-created as giant movements of men and forces. The dialogue was full of high-sounding philosophic discussion. When I saw the finished product, I saw a picture that I might not have written if I could have had my own way with the material. A screen writer is not a completely independent creative artist: he must be part of a team and often submerge his own ideas for the good of the final product. A big budget may sometimes be a handicap in turning out a good commercial picture, because production values may smother the story and the characters.

Each novel is a problem unto itself when being adapted for motion pictures; each screenplay must tell its own story in its own way. Movies must move; dialogue must be part of the story; the characters must be human enough for the audience to be able in some way to relate them to their own lives. A screenplay is always merely a link between the original story and the finished film.

I have found it best to plan on two or three great scenes of action in any screenplay and then to tell the rest of the story against simple sets. The average story is best told in normal surroundings.

And then, of course, to every screen writer there comes

the final test: has he written honestly good drama, re-created in the image of the original novel's author? Has he improved the original work? Has he really turned out a fine screenplay and given the director a great script that will bring in a big gross at the box office? He may not know the answers to these questions, but he does realize that no writer can survive the professionalism of this field whose work is merely just good enough, who has done a reasonable job at his craft, but who has not polished it a little more and added a bit of extra glow beyond studio demands, and whose life is not excited and enlarged by the reaction of many strangers to the job he has tried to do.

It is important that the screen writer knows, when he takes a novel to adapt to the screen, just what dangers he will face after he has completed his work, and plans for these eventualities. For making movies is not at all like the lonely art of writing a novel: it is a group effort, with many minds, many heads, and many voices—all having a part in its acceptance or rejection before it goes into actual production.

Even though you may, at times, think the reward does not always make the effort worth while, you will still keep trying, if you are a professional screen writer.

FRANK S. NUGENT

The Opening Scenes

The problem of the opening faces us all—newspapermen, fiction writers, nonfiction writers, dramatists. The newspaper formula is reasonably well established: the four W's: Who, What, Where, and When. "John Smith, 28, of Peoria, Ill., was killed yesterday when the plane he was piloting crashed and burned in a field outside Teaneck, N. J."—simple, direct journalism, but scarcely dramatic writing.

Alfred Hitchcock once expressed the problem this way: "The question is how to apply glue to the seat of the audience's trousers." He went on to say that he invariably considered a dozen obvious ways of opening his pictures, then discarded them all for one that was not obvious. This is all interesting, but not too helpful. What may strike Hitchcock as obvious may not seem at all so to his audience.

Perhaps even before considering the problem of the opening, we should ask what is meant by "story." The best definition I know is that a story is the upsetting of the *status quo*. In short, there is a situation or a condition; something happens to disturb it; the disturbance is the story; and the story ends when another *status quo* is attained, when life again reaches a state of balance.

20

For example, *The Caine Mutiny* begins by describing life aboard the *Caine* under an easygoing but effective skipper. Enter Captain Queeg, a petty martinet and a psychotic, and life aboard the *Caine* is subjected to almost seismic disturbances culminating in a mutiny, a court-martial, the breaking of Queeg, and ultimately the restoration of another balance.

Picnic is the study of a small town and some of the people in it. A new character is introduced, an irresponsible ne'er-do-well, whose personal chemistry sets off a chain of explosions: a sister rivalry flares into the open, and out of one girl's heartbreak comes a new understanding; an engagement is broken and a new love born; a spinster schoolteacher suddenly fights desperately for marriage. The story ends with the ne'er-do-well leaving town. Life settles back, but not quite the same as before.

Basically, a story amounts to the introduction of a new element into a given situation. It can be the new marshal riding into the Western town. It can be the new teacher taking over a classroom in *The Blackboard Jungle*. It can be Bing Crosby reporting for duty to the old parish priest in *Going My Way*. It can be the idealistic professor of law coming to grips with the grubby realities of a murder case in *Trial*. It can be the arrival of a glory-hunting cavalry officer at *Fort Apache,* where the paths of glory lead but to a massacre of his command. Or it can be the pressure of a storm, a flood, or a Mau-Mau uprising upon a group.

On the practical level, then, and reverting to the problem of an opening, I should say that the writer's first job is to look long and hard at his story and to see whether it can be reduced to terms of the upsetting of the *status quo*. What is the established situation? What is the new element that affects it? What is the end result? The process should not concern itself with details of the story—"and then he meets this girl, but her brother doesn't like him because they once had a fight . . ." The writer should examine the theme, not the story line. When the theme has been determined,

21

the problem of the opening reduces itself to two alternatives: the writer may begin either by establishing the existing situation or by introducing the new element. *The Caine Mutiny,* *Marty,* and *On the Waterfront* are examples of the former; *Picnic, The Blackboard Jungle,* and *Going My Way* illustrate the latter.

Obviously there are no hard and fast rules. No two writers will begin a story in exactly the same way. My preference, however, is to begin with the newcomer or the new element. My preceptor in this has been John Ford, four-time Academy Award winner for direction, for whom I have written several scripts. Ford once pointed out that among the earliest studies of figures in motion were the Leland Stanford photographs of a running horse. "A running horse," he said, "remains one of the finest subjects for a movie camera." It is no accident that most Ford pictures open with a figure in motion—it may be a stagecoach or a horseman in a Western; or, if the framework happens to be other than Western, a train pulling into a station, a river boat chugging toward an African dock, a bus dropping a passenger off at an Oklahoma crossroads.

Preston Sturges once composed his own rules for writing screenplays. One of them was: "An arrival is better than a departure." Ford thinks so too—his pictures usually begin with an arrival. It is a sound theory. Any arrival is interesting, including that of the new family next door, the new teacher, the new boss, the new clergyman, or the man with the sinister scar on his left cheek. "What's he up to?" asks the audience. Mr. Hitchcock would answer that the glue has just been applied to the seats of the audience's pants.

Since this is a book of trade secrets, I might as well confess that most of my screenplays employ the same opening technique. In *The Quiet Man* the opening shots are of a train rolling into a station, a lanky American alighting and asking the way to Inishfree—a simple enough request, but one that obviously piques the curiosity of porters, stationmaster, conductor, local fishwife, and of course the audience.

Soon it is shown that this is an Irish-born American who has come home to his mother country in search of quiet and peace. And what happens? He disturbs the *status quo*, to put it mildly. That was the story, and that was the technique.

The opening of *Three Godfathers* is as blunt as a hammer blow. Three bewhiskered horsemen pull up a trail to a hill-top overlooking a town. In three sentences it is established they have come to rob the bank. The first person they meet in town is an affable old codger in galluses, pruning his rose-bushes. They pause for a cup of coffee and some small talk. And then the old codger slips into his vest—with a bright silver star on it—and mentions his name, Perley Boone. It is the name that almost gives one of the gunmen heart failure—Perley is the toughest sheriff in the country. The story begins.

Of course we could have opened with the town and with the sheriff, establishing him for what he is, and we could have brought in the outlaws a full reel later. But, by opening with motion, with an arrival, and with the promise of exciting things to come, we had the story off to a quicker and more interesting start.

Alan LeMay's novel *The Searchers* opens suspensefully. A Texas homesteader cautiously steps off his porch and prowls a short distance over the prairie. He keeps low, and his eyes are narrowed and questing. He notes the sudden flight of a covey of quail; he hears a bird call in one quarter and its sharp answer from another. Then he suddenly runs back to barricade his homestead and arm his family against the still-unseen Comanche raiders. The setting sun is blood red where it strikes the house.

It seemed a perfect opening, just as it stood, with motion, suspense, terror. Ford and I discussed it for days, and then decided to hold back the scene. The picture opens, as so many Ford pictures have, with the lone horseman riding in—he's a dour figure, the brother of the steadfast home-steader. He has been away for some time, and for reasons only faintly touched upon. Was he a highwayman, soldier of fortune, adventurer? Was he in love with his brother's wife? Why did he seem to hate the "found boy" who had grown up in his brother's household? The picture never answered all the questions. We never meant that it should. But we drew a character of interest and speculation, and we met a family that was to be massacred or taken captive in the next reel or two. But when you look at it closely, you will see that we had been employing the time-honored technique; we had begun in motion, with an arrival, and we had established the *status quo* that soon was to be upset by a Comanche raid.

The opening can be as simple as that. Sometimes.

ELIHU WINER

TV—*Live or Film?*

Ideally, a story should be told in the precise length that is most effective and in the single medium that is most logical. But just as the requirements of television networks for split-second cut-ins coast to coast usually make arbitrary demands on the length of the story, so do problems of production often affect the form, live or film, in which a story will finally be shown.

Since such considerations are usually beyond the control of the writer, he obviously cannot establish precise criteria for the choice of live or film at the time of writing. He can, however, explore each method of storytelling in terms of strengths and weaknesses, scope and limitations, and perhaps draw certain general conclusions about the aptness of each in relation to any given story.

Obviously a film for television has a greater physical range than a live show, just as a film for theatrical exhibition has a greater physical range than a play in a legitimate theater. The filmed story can wander in time and space as no live story can, since the image is on a roll of film that can be edited, re-created, and eventually reproduced, whereas the electronic camera sends out an image that is dissipated at the instant of impact.

A character in a motion picture can walk from one sequence directly into another in a complete change of costume and make-up; he can age thirty or forty years in a single change of scene, or he can lose as many in a flashback. A film sequence can show a herd of thundering oxen charging directly at the viewer; it is true that a "live" camera can be placed in front of such a thundering herd, but it is not likely that the oxen will charge on cue and in the context of a story. Further, the process of rerecording (or dubbing, as it is commonly known in motion pictures), in which a number of sound tracks are blended into a final single track, makes it possible to photograph scenes of violent action with the highly mobile silent movie camera and to add sound later as the individual scene is edited into its proper place in the story.

In contrast to these and other advantages of film, the live-action story offers immediacy and a sense of participation to the viewer. In spite of such photographic devices as the cut, the moving shot, and the close-up, which have heretofore been confined to film, the live show is essentially closer to the legitimate stage than it is to the motion picture. The photographic devices add a dimension—they do not change the character of the living performance.

In brief, a motion picture is edited after the completion of photography. A live show is edited in advance of and during photography. The art of the television film is similar to the art of any other motion picture: it is the art of montage, the juxtaposition of photographed images into a filmic time that may bear no relation to the time of actual photography. Live television, on the other hand, bears an intrinsic relationship to the time of photography: the viewer sees the image at the precise instant that the camera does.

Once this essential difference between the two media is grasped, certain fundamental principles of dramatic storytelling become self-evident. For example, a story that ranges widely over time and space, that involves many characters or crowd scenes, or that calls for outdoor action that is believable to the eye is better told on film. A story that is tight and intensely dramatic and that involves few people in limited settings is told to better advantage in live action.

Occasionally I have written film shooting scripts for stories that cried for live production, and scripts for live production that would have benefited by the wider range of the motion picture.

At times, however, medium and story have coincided so completely that I found it difficult to think of any other way of telling the story for television. An example is the half-hour adaptation I wrote of a story by F. Scott Fitzgerald, "Three Hours between Planes." The original is structurally simple, involving only two people in a situation that starts out gracefully, almost lyrically, and then gradually develops into one of extreme tension. A man in his early thirties finds himself in the airport of a small Midwestern town with a three-hour wait between planes. He had lived in the town as a child, but had not been back for twenty years. On a wild impulse he calls a girl he had known when he was twelve and she was ten. The girl invites him to her house for a drink.

These preliminaries take only a few paragraphs in the story, and a very few minutes in the script. Both story and script are concerned mainly with the scene in which the boy and the girl play out a brief, impassioned moment that neither is likely ever to forget.

In the script, this scene takes up approximately twenty-two minutes of dialogue with no other characters present. Although such scenes are common in the legitimate theater, they are infrequent in theatrical motion pictures or in television, live or film. I suppose the scene could be played on film, but I doubt that its impact would ever match that of any of the three live productions of the script.

The reason for this is fairly obvious. A film is shot in bits and pieces—a page or two of dialogue, then a pause for a new camera setup, perhaps a reverse angle on the pages already shot, then another setup, and so on. Under these conditions no two actors could possibly create and sustain the emotional flow and the interplay of character that the scene demands. Although the story is simple in structure, it is intensely complex in emotional overtones. The creative skills of a sensitive film director and an expert film editor are of course helpful, but the convincing portrayal of complex emotions is primarily the responsibility of the actors. Camera tricks, overdramatic lighting, and unnecessary sound effects would be superfluous in the given circumstances.

A different problem presented itself recently when I made a one-hour adaptation of Edward Everett Hale's *The Man without a Country* for a live production.

Hale's story involves a large cast of characters and contains party sequences, a court-martial, and scenes at sea, including a naval battle. In addition, it covers a period of some sixty years. Yet, faced with the necessity of telling this story in a script, the production of which would be confined to a live studio, and further limited by the requirements of the "cameo" technique devised by producer Albert Mc-Cleery, I found that *The Man without a Country* could be told adequately within these physical limitations, using only six actors with full speaking parts and five others with less than fifty words each.

Inevitably such compression called as much for logistical ingenuity as for writing skill. The court-martial scene was reduced to two speaking parts, those of the presiding officer and of Philip Nolan, the story's protagonist. The naval battle was discarded. The party scenes could perhaps have used greater elaboration than was possible. The scene on deck in which Philip Nolan reads from Scott's *Lay of the Last Minstrel* would have been more effective if it had been possible to show the effect of the reading on the young officers of the ship. The scene in which a party of African slaves freed by an American ship plead to be allowed to return to their homes would have been more moving with many slaves than with the single spokesman I was able to use.

In spite of these and other limitations, the television production of *The Man without a Country* was faithful in spirit and in most details to the Hale story. To judge from its reception, it also had emotional intensity and dramatic impact.

In short, this was one way of telling *The Man without a Country:* a concentrated, highly personal version of the original. Some day I want to write an adaptation for the screen, using the basic approach of the television script but enlarging on the scope of the action. The result might not be any better than the television production, but it would be considerably different.

On one assignment I wrote both a film version and a live version of the same story, an original called *The Bounty Court-Martial.* The producers of the program use both live and film presentations, and were not certain which was to be the final form of this particular half-hour. At first I was asked to write the story for film and subsequently to adapt it for live performance. It was produced live.

The Bounty Court-Martial was based on the trial in 1792 of ten men accused of mutiny on April 28, 1789, on His Majesty's Armed Vessel *Bounty,* then under the command of Lt. William Bligh. Acknowledged leader of the mutiny was the first mate, Fletcher Christian, who had disappeared along with a number of the other mutineers. Of the ten men seized by a British ship in Tahiti, some were innocent of mutiny, some were guilty, but all were on trial for their lives.

Early in the preparation of this script I found it necessary to discard a strictly documentary approach, because the actual court-martial was undramatic. Bligh himself was not present, having been sent by the Admiralty back to the South Seas on another mission. Then too, the ten men on trial, including those obviously guilty, protested that they were really on Bligh's side, since this seemed the only way they could save their necks. A documentary account of what actually happened at the trial would have been dull and inconclusive. I decided, therefore, to take liberties with the facts and frankly to call the script fiction.

Oddly enough, the final result came nearer to the truth, as the hindsight of history allows us to know the truth, than a literal account of the court-martial could possibly have come. Although Bligh was not actually present at the trial, his malevolent spirit was there, because his accounts of the mutiny had poisoned the Admiralty and public opinion against the prisoners. And although none of the prisoners spoke out openly against Bligh at the trial, at least two did later: young ensign Peter Heywood and bosun's mate James Morrison. The latter's published accounts eventually turned public opinion against Bligh, whose reputation further suffered by involvement in another mutiny when he was governor of New South Wales in 1809. The matter has never been finally resolved—the literature is as pro-Bligh as anti-Bligh. Having to make a choice, however, I joined the anti-Bligh forces.

At this point, the very flexibility of the film medium began to betray me. Starting the script with a colorful opening aboard H.M.S. *Duke,* with officers, seamen, prisoners in chains, with cannons firing and trumpets blowing, I moved into the main saloon of the *Duke* for the court-martial itself. Using Peter Heywood as spokesman for the defense, I had the young ensign question Bligh about incidents that had taken place aboard the *Bounty* and that inevitably had led to the mutiny. As Bligh answered, I used that most commonplace and sometimes useful device, the flashback: I dissolved to the deck and cabins of the *Bounty,* and played out the scenes themselves.

This seemed the most logical way to tell the story. Actually, it proved disastrous. In the short space of a half-hour, minus time for commercials and credits, it was impossible to develop the scenes with any degree of dramatic interest. Further, the flashbacks, without furnishing any tension of their own, destroyed the tension that can always be expected in a courtroom drama. Finally, and most important, the protagonist and most interesting character of the flashback scenes turned out to be Fletcher Christian—and Fletcher Christian was not on trial.

The decision on the part of the producers to make a live show of *The Bounty Court-Martial* was not dictated by the quality of the film script. The decision resulted, however, in estimable benefit to the script and the production itself. Forced now to tell the same story in the confines of the main saloon of the *Duke,* I found the tension of a trial restored. The normal questions and answers about what had happened on the *Bounty* proved infinitely more dramatic than the scenes themselves. At the suggestion of the producers, I changed the spokesman from ensign Peter Heywood to bosun's mate James Morrison, to allow for more colorful speech in contrast to the elegant language of Bligh and of the presiding officer, Lord Hood. As in any good live production, the interplay among fine actors—Ronald Reagan as Morrison, the late Francis L. Sullivan as Bligh, and Raymond Massey as Lord Hood—provided an additional excitement that can come only under the stress of continuous action and actual performance.

I do not mean to rule out the possible effectiveness of a film treatment of this subject. For myself, though, I am satisfied that my live script was infinitely superior to my film version.

In each of the three instances I have mentioned, I seem to have wound up with a live production. I have also written a submarine story, *Fire One,* which could have been done only on film, and was; an adaptation of "The Celebrated Jumping Frog of Calaveras County," which should have been filmed, and was; and an adaptation of Henry James' "The Real Thing," which could have been either but was done on film, and might have been better live.

In short, a writer can only hope that the medium he gets will be right for his story.

New technical developments are steadily bringing live and film programs closer together in actual production. For example, three film cameras are sometimes used in the same way that live cameras are used to photograph continuous action, with their exposed film subsequently edited into a single reel of long shots, medium shots, close shots. Walt Disney has perfected the "Monster," an electronically operated film editor that speeds the process of editing the results of the three-film-camera technique to a point that brings filming very closely into line economically with live production. Dumont has developed the Electronicam, in which a single camera provides both a live and a film image, thus preserving the intimacy of a live show and at the same time ensuring a film image vastly superior to the ordinary kinescope recording, which is made by photographing the image on a picture tube.

As a writer who has worked in both film and live, I look on these and similar innovations with considerable suspicion and misgiving. It seems to me that the advantages of live and film are both striking and particular, and to attempt to use these advantages simultaneously is to negate them. The smoothness of film, its range and flexibility, its beauty of camera work in each individual shot and in the flow of shots—these and other qualities cannot be duplicated in live. On the other hand, film can never provide the intimacy, the sense of audience participation, the thrill of the shared experience of a good live show.

Finally, the recent development of a practical magnetic tape for capturing visual images has added one more variant to the storytelling techniques of television. At this writing, tape has been used only to replace kinescopes for delayed telecasting, with an occasional integration of a tape-recorded sequence of dramatic action in an otherwise live show. It is therefore much too early to do more than speculate on the possible use of tape in television, but there can be no doubt that, when it is perfected and in common use, tape will have a revolutionary effect on both live and film production.

The tape image on the home screen is far superior to that of film in definition, contrast, and depth, and is barely distinguishable from the live image. Tape would seem to have the flexibility of film in editing, and certainly it will be less expensive than film because the processing steps are eliminated and a single reel can be used over and over. Further, a tape recording of a live show may, because of the quality of its picture, give the viewer all the impact of a live show while allowing the correction of minor errors that sometimes mar a live performance. In short, tape would seem to provide a reasonable share of the best of both worlds.

The widespread use of tape does not seem imminent. In addition to the technical problems that have yet to be solved, there are practical problems of union jurisdiction that are certain to cause much discussion and inevitable delay. I am sure of one thing, however: at some point in the foreseeable future, this chapter will have to be revised, and it is then likely to be called, "TV—Tape, Live, or Film?" There may even come a time, if the advocates of tape are to be believed, when such a chapter will be altogether unnecessary, because there will be only one way to tell a story on television.

Religious and Biblical Films

For many years the Bible has tempted and challenged motion-picture makers. Where else can sin be exhibited in more lurid primal colors? Where else in all literature do the sacred and the profane exist in closer proximity? From orgy to revelation, the sound and silent cameras have turned the pages of scripture, punishing sin—but not before it has been examined with justifiable frankness worthy of eternal damnation.

A writer may be called upon to dramatize and expand scripture into a mammoth morality play, or to work in the documentary confines of some particular church group. In any event he will be confronted with problems that differ from all his past writing experience.

The basic difference of course is that in the field of religion the writer will be dealing with the great truths of faith. The fundamentalist unquestioningly accepts the word of the Bible as meaning what it says. The writer cannot rewrite the Bible. He may add to it where sections of narrative are incomplete. He may even subtract, in the sense of omitting material that is not relevant to the story he is telling. But he cannot change the basic story the Bible tells.

34

Many of the great Bible stories have "dark areas." A man is born, and then many years of his life are omitted; nothing is mentioned of what happened in this period. Perhaps through the ages some transitional passages have been lost. Perhaps meanings may have been changed through countless translations and interpretations. The modern writer can fill these empty spaces—not by pure invention, but by prowling through the artifacts of recorded archaeology. He may find clues that will help to supply the missing pieces, without changing the over-all meaning of the Biblical narrative. When the writer is filling in the missing areas and supplying the connecting experiences in the missing years, he must tread carefully, leaning heavily upon additional source material.

Bible dictionaries, encyclopedias, geographies, guide books, and lexicons are widely available. Stories of the Bible are told and retold in many literary, historical, and sacred works. The Koran and Midrash Rabbah supply missing episodes in the life of Moses; so do the great historians of antiquity—Philo, Josephus, Eusebius of Caesarea, among others. Every tomb that is opened, every scroll that is unearthed, adds to the sum total of historical information.

One small clue from the archaeologist Breasted enabled us, while working on the screenplay of *The Ten Commandments*, to describe the dramatic relationship of Moses, Rameses II, and the Princess Nefertiti. According to Breasted, the name of a certain Egyptian prince had been methodically obliterated from certain monuments and cartouches. This started a chain of conjecture among us. Could the erased name have been that of Moses? Many clues fitted, but our job was not to authenticate history but to justify dramatic invention. The Bible itself has only a single sentence on Moses' Egyptian upbringing (Acts 7:22): "And Moses was learned in all the wisdom of the Egyptians . . ." From such a slender springboard we developed a dramatic sequence that completed, without violating, the Biblical saga.

In the motion picture *Samson and Delilah* we needed a

transition between the magnificent beginning and conclusion supplied by the Bible. According to the Book of Judges, Samson sees a wealthy Philistine merchant's daughter in Timnath and arranges to marry her. At the wedding, the bride betrays Samson by revealing the answer to a riddle. Anxious to placate the enraged Samson, the bride's father offers his younger daughter instead. Samson refuses the offer. After burning the fields of the Philistine, he becomes an outlaw. The Bible picks up the narrative years later, in another time and place, with a completely new set of characters. Delilah offers, for a suitable remuneration, to trap the marauding outlaw. All details of their tragic romance are magnificently told—but what have Delilah and this great third act to do with Samson's interrupted marriage to the merchant's daughter?

So we writers began our search. This time the answer came from a simple piece of invention. Give the younger sister in Timnath a name, and every motive falls into place. Give her a name, and the story becomes a taut narrative in which every step builds inevitably in mounting drama toward the final climax. Call the rejected girl: Delilah! And since the Bible does not call her anything else, why should we not take this license?

Other experiences in trying to prepare screen stories based on Biblical characters were not always so successful. For example, the story of Solomon and the Queen of Sheba has challenged writers for many years. The wisest and wealthiest king on earth entertains a beautiful and exotic visitor. She matches his wit with riddles, and his riches jewel for jewel from her fabulous caravan, so wonderfully described in II Chronicles 9:1.

On the surface the situation seemed to offer everything, but there were a few traps and mirages. A succession of writers worked on this subject for a long time. Perhaps "wisdom" in a hero does not photograph as well as biceps. We were finally on our way to getting a good script when an Italian picture company got the same story to the screen before we did. Their *Solomon and Sheba* may not have lived up to the expectations we had for ours, but it was in the theaters before ours was out of the typewriter.

Salome is another fascinating lady for a screen story. All we had to do was to justify that unpleasant moment when the lecherous Herod fulfilled her extraordinary request for the Prophet's head on a platter. The screenplay took rather daring liberties with the event. The finished movie proved to be a critical failure, but was financially successful. In spite of a lack of critical enthusiasm for some of our Biblical pictures, there are likely to be many more.

Not only major studios, but many small companies as well, frequently produce religious pictures. Some of the latter offer the free-lance writer interesting and lucrative assignments; many consider original material that might fit into their programs. The following is a list of a few of these companies: Cathedral Films, Family Films, J.K.F. Films, Broadcasting and Film Commission, World Wide Pictures, Great Commission Films, Moody Bible Institute, Lutheran Church Productions, Methodist Radio and Film Commission, Paul Hurd, Allen Shilin, Centurian Films, Catholic Movies, Fair Deal Motion Picture Service, Catholic Motion Picture Enterprises, and Foundation Films.

In the theatrical field, Century Films stands high in activity. Centurian is preparing at least one film, budgeted at about $2,000,000. World Wide is connected with the evangelist Billy Graham.

I have worked on a number of documentary screenplays for the Lutheran Layman's League. Two of these were feature-length films in which information and doctrine were presented in simple dramatic stories for showing within Lutheran church groups. Lutheran representatives supplied the religious material and checked the screenplays for doctrine. The pictures were so well produced that several were released to the general public.

The continual growth of all church congregations offers a widening field of opportunities to the professional screen and television writer. The growing emphasis on quality means increasing attention to the writing. Biblical dialogue is admittedly difficult to write. The writer must achieve a suitable balance between the language of King James and the living effectiveness of modern speech.

The stories of the Bible are never old. Man's faith is never dated. The legends and hero sagas of the ages redramatized in each generation have the power to fire the imagination. It is the staff that brings forth water from rocks, that opens seas, that leads nations to freedom. The writing of religious screen material is rewarding for any author with faith in the written word.

The Western

Until 1934 my lack of interest in the American West was boundless—I had not even *read* a Western story, much less had I tried to write one. Then, in December, 1934, I wrote two Western short stories, more or less in desperation, and sold both of them.

Earlier that year I had arrived in New York with the manuscripts of some twenty mysteries. After trying my luck at countless editorial offices, and getting an equivalent number of rejections, I finally met a sympathetic editor who suggested I try my hand at a couple of Westerns. Since that time, deep in the Depression with my hotel rent six weeks overdue, I have been active in the Western field: short stories, novels, screenplays, television scripts.

After writing Westerns for some time, with little if any real knowledge of the West, I decided to do some research. At the suggestion of Ernest Haycox, probably the most accomplished of all Western writers, I started accumulating my own library of Western history and biography. Then I traveled extensively in the West: I went to the home of Jesse James and met some of the James family; in New Mexico I talked to Charles and Frank Coe, who had actually ridden with Billy the Kid; I met partisans as well as detractors of famous outlaws; I talked to a few surviving old-time peace officers.

I acquired a love for the old West, which has never left me. But more important, I developed the habit of research. Today I read little Western fiction, but I do read all available factual books about the West.

Since those early days, the Western has become big business. Recently television has turned more and more attention to the so-called "adult" Western, until today producers of non-Western programs are concerned about their own fluctuating "ratings."

In 1956 the major studios produced fifty-four Westerns—one-third of their entire output; at the same time the independents made between thirty and forty Westerns—nearly half their output.

I have worked in Hollywood since 1942, when I sold a Western novel to the late Harry Sherman and received a six-week writing assignment. The first person I met in Hollywood exclaimed: "Oh, not another Western!"

On an average of four times a month for the past fifteen years I have heard the same remark, although sometimes an adjective is placed between "another" and "Western." However, for every complaint "Not another Western!" there has been another, sweeter refrain: *"No Western picture has ever lost money!"*

Fortunes and reputations have been made by the lowly Western. John Wayne was the top money-maker for many years. Most of his pictures have been Westerns.

Clark Gable, after half a dozen "important" turkeys, was becoming box-office poison. One Western, *The Tall Men,* put him back near the top. Gary Cooper, Gregory Peck, Robert Taylor, James Stewart, Alan Ladd, and other screen luminaries of the first magnitude have done extremely well with Westerns.

Many a studio has lost money on two- and four-million-dollar "important" and "significant" pictures, only to recoup such losses with a Western or two. *Shane* grossed $16,000,000 for Paramount; Howard Hughes' *The Outlaw* and David Selznick's *Duel in the Sun* did about as well.

Yes, but how long is the Western trend going to last? A long time, in spite of "Oh, not another Western!" Westerns will be around for a good many years; in fact the Western trend is still on the upgrade.

In the past few years the major studios have lost nearly all their stars as well as their most important producers and directors—they have "gone independent." At a major studio a producer may take a chance on a theme or story—it is the studio's money he is risking. Let him leave the studio, however, and he wants to play it safe. There is nothing safer than a Western.

Most of the big stars now have their own "capital-gain" production companies. Frequently, in return for full financing, they agree to make one picture a year for the studio. For the studio they will do an "important" or a "significant" picture; for their own company they may do only Westerns.

More big-budget Westerns are being made today than at any time in motion-picture history, and will continue to be made as long as independent producers and stars feel that they must play it safe.

Another new trend is becoming increasingly apparent. The "B" pictures, almost discarded with the advent of the wide screen, are making a comeback. Twentieth Century-Fox contracted for "B" pictures in 1957, and the other major studios are negotiating for a series of similar pictures. Most of these small-budget films will necessarily be Westerns.

Today many Hollywood writers who formerly scoffed at Westerns are ransacking bookstores and libraries for "ideas" or to "absorb some Western atmosphere." Books that are enjoying a revival include *Wyatt Earp: Frontier Marshal*, by Stuart N. Lake; *The Saga of Billy the Kid*, by Walter Noble Burns; *The Rise and Fall of Jesse James*, by Robertus Love; *Triggernometry*, by Eugene Cunningham; *The Cow-*

boy, by Phillip Rollins. Then too, old copies of *Adventure, Short Stories, Ranch Romances,* and other pulp Western magazines are rapidly becoming collector's items. Radio and television writers have already bought most of the extant copies.

Writers who a few years ago could not distinguish between a pinto horse and a Navy Colt are today turning out "horse operas" for television and motion pictures. The Beverly Hills and Hollywood Cadillac dealers can testify to their success.

Before World War II, Western stories had a certain popularity in magazines but were at an all-time low as books. From 1929 until 1942 the average Western novel sold less than 2,000 copies. One of mine, published in 1939, sold 1,850 copies; another, in 1941, sold 1,900 copies; a third, in 1942, sold about the same. Each of the three was reprinted by Grosset and Dunlap, and each sold another 1,500 copies.

Before 1942 a writer's total income from a Western novel was often less than $500 unless he had a market for serial rights; few writers had such a market. For example, a certain writer had a contract with a publisher for six Western novels a year for a flat fee of $150 per book. The movies bought few Western novels before the war. For each of these few, from $250 to $750, rarely as much as $1,000, was paid.

Then came the war and the advent of the paper-backs. Soon the publishers had scraped the bottom of the barrel in mysteries and, desperate for stories, decided to try a few Westerns. They sold well. The Council of Books in Wartime included a few Western books in the Armed Services Editions, and discovered that these were the most popular of all their items.

By the end of the war, Westerns were selling as well as any other kind of paper-back—a publisher could expect to sell 100,000 copies. The market for Westerns remained steady until about 1947, when publishers began increasing their print orders of Westerns—and selling them. Overnight, Westerns became runaway best sellers. By 1950 they were selling 20 per cent better than mysteries.

In 1956, more than 300,000,000 paper-backs of all kinds were sold. Of these, approximately 100,000,000 were Westerns; 80,000,000 were mysteries; the rest, 120,000,000, included all the other categories.

The Western writer, who formerly was fortunate if he earned $500 from a novel can now get *advances* of as much as $7,000.

Sales of 200,000 and 300,000 copies of a Western novel are commonplace. The top writers double that figure, sometimes reaching the million mark. And Westerns do not die. Publishers continue to reissue them, as long as they sell. Owen Wister's *The Virginian*, first published in 1902, has recently been reissued in hard covers. Zane Grey books with copyright dates of 1912, 1914, and 1916 are appearing in huge editions.

Edgar Allan Poe has often been called the father of the detective story. The father of the Western cannot be named as accurately. In general, however, Owen Wister is credited as having *revived* interest in the Western; he bridged the transition from the wild and woolly dime novel to the modern Western. More than any other writer, however, Zane Grey popularized the Western novel. His *Riders of the Purple Sage,* is widely considered the best Western novel ever published. A half dozen other Zane Grey novels are also highly regarded, but his last works fall considerably below present-day standards.

A more recent Western writer, Ernest Haycox, is generally regarded as the most accomplished. His writing technique, developed in the pulps, was vastly superior to that of Zane Grey. The characters in his stories were adult, intelligent people. He had carefully studied the West, and his stories had a flavor and authenticity never before found in Western stories. His typical hero, "the Hamlet of the plains" was well represented in movie performances by John Wayne and

Gary Cooper. John Wayne, indeed, became an overnight star after appearing in *Stagecoach,* based on Haycox's short story, "Stage to Lordsburg." Haycox, who died in 1950, at the early age of fifty-one, wrote some 24 novels and about 250 short stories. All his books have had enormous sales, and are still being reissued.

Max Brand (one of fourteen pseudonyms of the most prolific writer of all time, Frederick Faust) enjoys a great popularity among Western fans; writers do not regard him so highly. He created a fantasy West that never existed, and his characters, mostly philosophical freebooters who just happened to appear in Western stories, do not typify the genuine Western hero.

Western novels by current writers are today in great demand in Hollywood, bringing as much as $15,000 for screen rights. Within the past three years, as a matter of fact, individual Western novels have sold for $60,000.

The Western "original," which is a treatment or synopsis of a story, is not selling well. Producers have learned that Westerns in synopsis form are rather useless, because so much depends upon the characterizations, the actual bits of business, incidental material. Complete shooting screenplays, however, move briskly at good prices, although not quite as good as for published novels. Original Western screenplays sell. What sweeter refrain is there for a professional writer?

Comedy

The demand for good comedy has always been greater than the supply, because comedy writing is a specialized and difficult craft.

My conversations with student-writer groups indicate strongly that the majority of aspiring comedy writers do not really want to know how to *write* comedy—they want to know how to *sell* it. For the benefit of that majority, I shall begin with that aspect of comedy.

My best advice is: get your material into the hands of a theatrical agent. An agent gets 10 per cent of anything he sells (or leases), and he is always on the lookout for new writers capable of writing laughs. Any writer's magazine contains lists of theatrical agents. (Do not confuse them with literary agents, who charge fees for reading and criticizing your work.) Do not send unsolicited manuscripts to comedians, networks, or advertisers. Chances are that anything you do submit will be returned unread because of the possibility of lawsuits.

The most certain avenue to selling comedy is through a comedian or his own writers. Unless you live in Hollywood or New York, your chances of meeting a major star are, of course, slim.

45

I was in California when I decided to try writing comedy for a living. I went to a broadcasting studio in an effort to see Eddie Cantor. Although I could not get past the doorman, I did meet Howard Snyder, who, with Hugh Wedlock, was writing Cantor's show at the time. Wedlock and Snyder gave me my first opportunity to write radio comedy.

Later I was in a position to encourage other young people who accosted me in much the same way as I had first met Wedlock and Snyder. Some of these young writers have gone on to great success.

When I was writing for the early George Gobel on television, I received one of the funniest letters I have ever read: a housewife wanted a chance to write comedy. We let her spend one season sitting in with us and contributing to our scripts. I am sure that Mary Agnes Liddell will eventually write a successful book or play.

Harry Winkler, now a firmly entrenched comedy writer in television, also began on the Gobel show. Earlier, in Chicago, Winkler had met Gobel when the latter was a local performer. Gobel used some of Winkler's material in his act. When television beckoned, Gobel brought Winkler to California.

These biographical notes are cited to make a point: personal contact is your best wedge. In every metropolitan area some young comedian is at work in a supper club, a hotel, stag dinner, charity affair, or church social. That young comedian (or tired old third-rater) needs material. Chances are that he cannot afford to buy material from established writers but will welcome the opportunity to buy, or lease, or steal something fresh and funny from a fresh and funny author. Once you have made contact with one performer, if you have anything at all to offer, you will be surprised at how quickly you will make other contacts through him.

Another avenue to commercial success is through the theater. Write a funny play, get it on Broadway, and you are established. Aside from the money the play itself will earn, movie studios, broadcasting networks, and agencies will all clamor for your services.

One final word about selling your material: you will find it easier to do if what you have to offer is genuinely original. Do not be imitative. Do not attempt to copy the style of an accepted success. Think differently, write differently, find new areas for comedy. It is not easy, of course, but if it were, this chapter would be unnecessary.

What makes comedy writing so specialized and so difficult? There are several reasons. Primarily, there is the audience.

With the possible exception of a political candidate in action, nothing turns an otherwise pleasant citizen into a carping, derisive critic so quickly as comedy in public entertainment. It requires almost as much insulation against abuse to write comedy as it does to stand for public office. When a writer sets himself up as an author of comedy, whether for television, motion pictures or the theater, he is unintentionally inviting insults, because the individual appreciation of comedy is even more specialized than writing it. What makes one man laugh may elicit a groan from another. Therefore the preparation of comedy material for mass entertainment must cover as broad a basic appeal as possible; this accounts for the critical opinions concerning the low estate to which even many professional people believe comedy has sunk.

If comedy has reached the low estate many professional and lay critics contend, much of the blame can be laid at their feet, for these same nay sayers are often in the vanguard of the hordes pressing for constraining censorship. In addition to being bound by the Motion Picture Code and the broadcasting networks' continuity acceptance departments, comedy writers have had to exercise increasing self-imposed censorship to avoid the slings and arrows of outraged audience components.

Would it surprise you to know that if the writer makes a joke about flowers he had better be careful how he does it? Camellia lovers are organized! Used-car dealers, a natural target for humor, will fight back at writers through lawyers' letters. Real-estate men will make angry telephone calls. The nation's dry element will run screaming to the press if you imply that whiskey is associated with bliss; distillers will snarl if you imply that whiskey is the root of all evil. Friends of politicians will hurl harpoons via Western Union. Press agents will defend actors. Loyal employees will defend corporations. Police will defend themselves. Nobody will defend the writer.

A comedy writer will be pilloried, lashed, whipped, bludgeoned. But the rewards will be worth the welts. Apart from the handsome fees he will collect for his work, he will experience the exhilaration that comes only when an audience erupts in laughter at something he has written. It is a sudden burst of glory that illuminates his being, and it lasts all the way out to the lobby, where the comedian may be seen being congratulated for "rising above the material."

There is more truth than cynicism in this last statement. A recurrent problem facing the commercial humorist is that of convincing producers, directors, and actors that what has been committed to paper is funny. Comedy is so personal that its interpretations are many, varied, and frequently frustrating to the author. Complete accord on comedy values is seldom achieved among all concerned with a project until after it has been completed and the end product exposed to the final jury. If the audience responds with laughter, the writer has succeeded; if the audience does not laugh, the author has failed. Comedy is not what makes *you* laugh; it is what makes *the most people* laugh.

When I first began writing jokes for radio, in 1938, I was told by my superiors that I was writing for an audience with a twelve-year-old mentality. Since those apprentice years, the American audience has either grown intellectually or, like Mark Twain's father, has learned a lot in a few years.

A number of producers of unsuccessful screen comedies still cling to archaic ideas. These men work, of course, in an industry where personal success may be built on a series of failures, if they have had large enough budgets. One of their strongest beliefs is that it takes more than one man to write a comedy.

As long as there is a predominance of thinking along these lines, it might be well for anyone who wants to write laughter to find a collaborator. Sooner or later the writer will be forced into a collaboration in the preparation of screen or broadcast material, and he should find someone who complements his own talents and personality. If one is going to write comedy, he might as well be happy doing it. Contrary to the popular conception of comedy writers, they are not a morose group. Most of my close friends are comedy writers, and they are the happiest group I know.

These men have one thing in common: a point of view and an ability to express it. Apart from their training and experience, this is what makes them successful writers. They passed through that era of the eclectic gag man, learning the hard way how to string jokes together, how to blend gags into dialogue with sure brevity, how to build a situation and a character.

In 1938 or earlier, a man sat down at his typewriter to compose a spot for a comedian, and decided he would do a routine of farm jokes; today he spends more time thinking of some aspect of farm life, and then, with a point of view in mind, explores that one aspect. He may read a magazine article about the rise in farm income. He decides that a portrait of a wealthy farmer might lend itself to some fun. He gets a joke about a farmer plowing while wearing a full-dress suit. By exercising more imagination, he asks himself what happens to the old dress suits farmers wear out? Scarecrows. He toys with that notion, and finally settles down to write a sketch about a man who earns his living in a rural area as an exclusive scarecrow's tailor.

Perhaps the foregoing is an oversimplification of the

changes that have occurred in comedy writing, but a number of writers eking out a living have either failed to understand those changes or are incapable of updating their own thinking. These are men who are no more than "gag men"; given a situation they can think of a joke, a funny line, or a comical piece of business. Once the Hollywood stages and radio studios teemed with gag men; today they are rare for the simple reason that comedy itself has changed.

To survive today, the comedy writer must have a point of view and the ability to express it, as I have said before. To express a point of view, the writer must be able to create gags and to understand the basic rules of dramatic construction, characterization, and dialogue. The artist who draws a good caricature knows anatomy, bone structure, and muscle placement: the pointing up of these features makes him a good caricaturist. The same is true in comedy: a few deft lines of dialogue tell us more about a character or situation than pages of description. Today's comedy writer is a caricaturist with a thorough understanding of his subject matter. He has an eye and ear for the mores of our civilization, a nose for news, compassion, education, and someone to write *for.*

Unless the writer and his comedian share a point of view or understand each other's intellect, they are robbing each other and cheating their audience. At one point in my own career, before I was aware of this contention, I did some writing for a friendly man with the improbable name of Pinky Lee. Good performer though Mr. Lee was, he never understood what I was attempting to do; in all fairness, I must admit that although I had an inkling of what he wanted, I could not understand why. Lee and I seldom saw eye to eye, and I was as woefully inadequate in his mind as he remains in mine. After a harrowing period of thirteen weeks, I was relieved of my duties. I had learned a lesson I hope I will always be able to afford remembering: never write for money alone.

It is vital to the success of a writer that he write only

for those people he understands and who understand his work. The men for whom I have written comedy with some success all share a common facet—their approach is cerebral, they have an *attitude* toward life—Bing Crosby, Ed Wynn, George Gobel. Their attitudes are not all the same, to be sure, but they are men who are positive in their beliefs and understand what they are doing. I also believe they understood what I was doing, and as a result my associations with all three were happy ones.

Knowing your actors is half the battle. Sometimes it is more. The writer who knows his actors better than any man in the business is undoubtedly Freeman Gosden, the co-creator of Amos 'n Andy. For many years Gosden and Charles Correll wrote their own scripts. When they did bring in writing help, I eventually served a season on their staff. It was fruitful for me, because I learned a great deal from two acknowledged masters of the situation comedy form.

One day we were sitting in the office, concentrating on an entrance line for the Kingfish. Four writers tossed off one suggestion after another, none of which was acceptable. In desperation, I turned to Freeman and said, "Exactly what would the Kingfish say himself if he were to walk into this room right now?" Freeman shifted his mind into blackface, dropped his voice a notch, and rumbled out a line that amused us all. I do not recall what it was, but it went into the script. I do recall that I marveled at the fact Freeman Gosden knows his characters so well that it is ridiculous for anyone to try to compete with him in writing them.

By training himself to think in the idiom of the performers he is writing for, the writer can make his job easier. Working on the Crosby shows, we wrote for every major talent in show business. Whenever we had a guest with a distinctive style, voice, or mannerisms, our job was always easier. Durante was a dream to write for: we could spit out lines in raspy voices that seemed to fit. Groucho Marx was a stimulating pleasure; we could twist almost any common statement into a Marxism, then top it with irreverence. Clifton Webb's precise, knifelike delivery; Beatrice Lillie's equally keen precision; Jimmy Stewart's warm, fumbling manner; Jack Benny's delicious character delineation—all these people are so much easier to write for than the run-of-the-mill guest actor, because we know what these performers stand for in the public's eye.

Popular comedians, in broadcasting, motion pictures, and the theater, have already established their characters and points of view. By the time a new writer is assigned to do a script for any comedy star, he will find a pattern already set; his chore will be that of searching for variations on the established theme.

Television's voracity is forcing the medium to discover and develop new personalities for itself (and all phases of show business); there is hopeful indication that new points of view will arrive with them. Chances are that the older, more permanently established free-lance comedy writers will be given first crack at the new arrivals. But each new personality will have some young writer in his background, and that newcomer should move in with him to work with more experienced authors.

The most perfect correlation between creative writer and creative performer was realized in the person of one man: Fred Allen. Nobody could write for him as well as he could himself. (Nobody, I might add, could write comedy as well as Fred Allen.) The sincere student of contemporary comedy writing should make the study of Fred Allen's work an absolute must in his curriculum. Allen's lifetime was devoted to broadening the fields of his own experiences by reading, talking, listening, and looking, including as much universality as possible in order to find humor in areas where others had not explored and exploited.

Those areas exist.

Life today is so changing, so rapidly paced, that each day seems to offer a new frontier for the exploration of humor.

Civilization offers constant challenges for the writer. Even the search for it inspired Dr. Albert Schweitzer to answer an interviewer: "Civilization? I think it's a wonderful idea; someone should start it."

Science Fiction

Since space satellites have become an accomplished reality, the whole realm of science fiction has taken on a new credibility in the eyes of the experts as well as of the general public.

A decade ago, Dick Tracy's wrist radio seemed altogether suitable to the somewhat juvenile vagaries of a comic strip. Today, tiny transistors make it an accomplished fact.

Fifty years ago, H. G. Wells wrote what were then termed "novels based on fanciful scientific speculation," such as *The Time Machine, The War of the Worlds, The Invisible Man, In the Days of the Comet,* and *War in the Air.* Almost a century ago, Jules Verne wrote "scientific romances with fantastic creations." Today, with so many of their "scientific speculations" having been turned into realities, their fictional "fantastic creations" do not meet with the same incredulity. In Jules Verne's time a radio receiver might have seemed as fantastic as today's nebulous Unidentified Flying Objects. Now we place a radio inside a space missile and shoot it out to orbit around the earth. A few years ago, we may have wondered whether we should allow our children to watch TV shows about space cadets, rocket ships, disintegrator

54

guns, and guided missile service stations that, so it was claimed, hung in space with nothing to anchor them. Today, scientists believe an earth ship will make trips to the moon and to the planet Mars within the predictable future. In preparation for future space travel, the first lecture courses anywhere on Space Theory and Rocket Ship Technology have been given in San Francisco, Los Angeles, and San Diego. Among the learned faculty are such experts as Dr. Wernher von Braun, lecturing on The Exploration of Mars; Robert W. Buchheim, Lunar Flight; Krafft A. Ehricke, Interplanetary Operations; William H. Pickering, Guidance Techniques; Heinz Haber, Space Medicine—Physical Factors of the Space Environment; Dr. Hubertus Strughold, Space Environmental Factors; Samuel Herrick and Joseph W. Siry, Earth Satellites; John I. Shafer, Propulsion—Solid Rocket Design; Ernest E. Sechler, Structural Materials, Configurations, and Analyses; Alfred J. Eggers, Jr., Recovery Dynamics—Possibility of Non-Destructive Testing; L. M. K. Boelter and H. Guyford Stever, Why Space Technology?; and Herbert C. Corbin, Time Dilatation Effects in Space Travel.

The premise of science fiction as a new art form in movies, TV, radio, books, and magazines is simply that anything man is capable of imagining can happen. The imaginative word pictures conjured by authors can fire the creative talents of inventors, scientists, and engineers. Then, like wrist radio or a camera small enough to conceal in your hand, there it is—a reality and no longer fantastic.

Anything is possible in science fiction. This unique and fertile field is literally one market in which a producer or story editor may tell you that your story line is incredible or fantastic and mean that he likes it. Other kinds of fiction may find source material in past history or contemporary events; science fiction reaches into space and the future for its research.

Science fiction is here to stay; all indications are that this market will continue to expand in motion pictures and television. Writing in this field may become one of the most important forms of constructive literature within the next two decades.

Two basic qualities are requisite in the successful writer of science fiction: imagination and scientific curiosity. It goes without saying that he must have a solid basic understanding of science and familiarity with all its concepts. He must know, for example, the electrochemical nature of the brain and human nervous system, as well as the structure of the atom and the definition of the Einstein theory. Progress in medicine, aviation, ballistics, transportation, cybernetics, and automation must interest him. He must keep abreast of every development in the field of science, because he never knows when even an apparently insignificant item may spark a story for him.

There is a formula for science fiction literature, just as there is a pattern for all other types of writing. The writer can take any one of the basic plots and, by adding a fantastic new invention or an exciting but as yet unproved scientific theory, come up with a salable script. Science fiction is fantasy against a science background. The resolution of the plot explains the nature of the gimmick being used. It is almost as if the writer finds his gimmick, starts writing his story at the finish, and proceeds backward to the beginning.

Excellent examples of science fiction writing for television can be found in the Science Fiction Theater, a filmed series produced by Ziv. Poison gas is seeping along the roots of a "killer" tree in the desert. A scientist resolves the plot by determining that the gas is coming from the earth's center; he injects a tube by means of which he is able to photograph the interior of the earth. A couple from outer space are controlled electronically by their native planet. They escape to earth and take up residence near an electric power plant, which makes ineffective the other planet's electronic influence on the couple. Later the master generator in the nearby power plant explodes, and the couple disappears from the earth. Because of extrasensory perception and an accidental short-wave transmission via a television microwave, an innocent woman is suspected of being a spy when she is able to receive secret information being recorded on a dictating machine several blocks away. A giant reflector is used to direct certain devastating sun rays into a secret laboratory, thereby causing a mysterious explosion.

Science fiction comprises more than robots, mechanical men, or ordinary automation, but if a story can be strengthened by such additions so much the better.

An imaginative writer may place a human conflict against a background of outer space with the story conflict taking place inside a space ship or on a landing field poised strategically just beyond the earth's magnetic field or on another planet. Again he may plot an interstellar conflict and give it a human earthbound resolution.

A fantastic premise is vital to science fiction. The writer may evolve a story so fantastic he may think an editor will reject it as being scientifically questionable. The editor may do so if the background material has not been thoroughly researched, but a rejection on the basis of incredible premise is not likely. For example, a plot might concern a man dying of an incurable malady and agreeing to an experiment in which he will be frozen in a block of ice for three weeks. At the end of this time the ice is removed and the man is still alive. Such a fantastic premise must be made believable, possibly by emphasizing the fact that a medical scientist has made a lifelong study of animal hibernation and discovered that in hibernation the body temperature drops twenty to thirty degrees and that animals never contract disease in hibernation because bacteria remain dormant at such temperatures. He may have observed that fish are often frozen within the ice of their habitat, but are still alive when the ice melts.

Well-researched science fiction has achieved added popularity since the advent of man-made satellites. Writers whose talents lie in this direction may sell not only to TV and movies but also to magazines. They can lease rights for TV and movies, later using the same plots for magazine stories or novels.

The trend is now definite toward more science fiction in motion pictures. These productions are often low budget, which means easier and more numerous sales. It is not impossible to sell such a subject for an hour or ninety-minute TV program.

The writer who can make a soundly constructed teleplay or a screen original in science fiction will have no trouble getting an agent. Agents are in business to earn 10 per cent on the sales they make for writers. If scripts are commercial in content and treatment, an agent can sell them quickly. I doubt if anything pleases an agent more than fast—and repeat—sales of a client's literary material.

The writer who knows his background data in science and who keeps his imagination working overtime can turn out science-fiction scripts that will sell. Stories with a constructive premise command better prices, and also give the writer a greater satisfaction in his accomplishment. A prime example of high literary level in science fiction may be found in the prolific work of Ray Bradbury.

Yes, anything imaginable can happen in science fiction —even a writer who sells every script he writes, although the average professional writer might be inclined to think this kind of premise incredulous and altogether unbelievably fantastic.

Factual TV

The last—not always the most important—act of writing a factual television program is performed at the typewriter. The writer has no control over the materials he must put together: he cannot create character, or be consulted on casting, or insist that the rules of logic or the traditions of art govern his denouement.

In the field of the documentary, there are no rules, no accepted body of experience, no entrance requirements. Until recently, there was no market; the present market is limited. It follows that there can be no generalized survey of the field, certainly not by anyone who has worked in it. There can be only first-person narratives—this is mine.

In September, 1950, I asked an executive whether the National Broadcasting Company was ready with a special program marking the obviously impending victory of the United Nations forces in Korea. He said: "No. Why don't you do it?" So I spent my spare weekday hours in the *New York Times* library compiling a chronology, and my week ends in a film library looking at 16 mm film in a hand viewer. Then I wrote a script, and told the editors to cut the film to the script. We recorded a narration, and NBC News distributed to a group of its affiliates a film entitled "Victory in Korea." The next day the armies of Communist China crossed the Yalu River!

At the time I had been an employee of a broadcasting company for three months, but had never worked extensively with film before. On this project I spent about ten thousand dollars. I do not know whether what I learned was worth the money to NBC—it was to me.

I learned it is cheaper to cut 35 mm film and then reduce it to 16 mm than to reduce the whole film and then cut it. I learned that film can tell a story if properly edited, and that film should never be cut to script, but script should be written to film. I learned that film editing is a high skill, and that the tastiest phrase loses something when punctuated by artillery barrage.

Most important, I learned that if a man said he was experienced in this undefined field, no one could dispute it. No one could stop him; no one could help him. Since those days, there have been Edward R. Murrow's See it Now, Henry J. Salomon's Victory at Sea and Project 20, among others, but there is more an impression of activity in the field rather than any real upsurge.

If the program is all film, it follows the technical rules of a film documentary. If the program is all live television, then it becomes a lecture, possibly with slides and graphs. Television documentaries, it seems to me, should be built around a person of authority, and should use both live and film as tools of a new trade.

The NBC News camera chief in Germany, the Americanized Berliner Gerhardt (Gary) S. Stindt, is a good newsman to whom a story is a challenge. After the Berlin blockade, Gary became curious about what was going on behind the massive walls of Spandau prison in the British zone. Inside were the seven Nazis sentenced to prison at the Nürnberg trials: Hess, Raeder, Doenitz, Funk, and von Neurath. Gary scouted the area, and finally gained access to and use of a garret with direct line of sight into Spandau.

For six months he and an assistant spent time in that garret, watching the guards change, and taking pictures, with a long-focus lens, of unrecognizable activity inside the garden. They could see an iron door open and close, and dim figures in the garden. Until their film was developed, however, they did not know what they had—their camera lens was that much more powerful than their binoculars. Thousands of feet of developed film showed nothing more than guards going back and forth.

Stindt did not know what use could be made of his film. He sent it on, and we all looked at it—a few miserable figures, in GI overcoats dyed black, moving listlessly back and forth on the other side of a high wall. Stindt had to be brought back to New York to identify them. It was a journalistic coup: these were the top Nazis still alive. Many months later a date was set, and I was told to fill a half hour. We had Stindt's film, and four weeks during which neither I nor my film editors would be relieved of regular assignments.

Obviously, seven men halfheartedly pacing a yard is not a story. It is, if anything at all, the end of a story. For the next week we looked at German newsreels in our film library. The Germans, artists with the newsreel, were determined to record their infamies in pulsating, lifelike images. We divided our documentary into segments, each a newsreel shot juxtaposed with one inside Spandau. The program was called "The Road to Spandau."

Joseph C. Harsch, Washington reporter for the *Christian Science Monitor* and for some years a news commentator for NBC News, was assigned to the project as narrator.

Once we had edited the segments of film, the rest was easy. The story dictated the structure. We began with Spandau itself. The guards came and went—American, French, British, and Russian. We talked about Hitler, Goebbels, and Göring, and how they died, and about those who were hanged at Nürnberg. And these were the rest.

There were two kinds of Nazi war criminals: the hoodlum

and the technician. Both were present in Spandau. The chief hoodlum was Hess, who escaped hanging because he had flown to Britain to dictate peace before the worst of the crimes against civilization were committed. We had shots of Hess with Hitler in the 'twenties and 'thirties; Hess the rioter; Hess the collaborator in *Mein Kampf;* Hess administering to thousands of assembled Nazi officials the oath of personal allegiance to Hitler. Then cut to tall, gaunt figure in garden—Hess.

We showed Raeder, the man who built the German fleet, welcoming the *Deutschland* with Hitler as it brought back from Spain Germans who had died fighting for Franco; von Schirach at a youth rally with Hitler; raids on Jewish shops; Himmler at cages of prisoners on the Eastern front.

We wanted Himmler in the program, with the crematoria and the piles of children's shoes. Otherwise we should not be dealing with Nazism—only with seven miscellaneous men in flappy coats. We included Speer, because he was the least objectionable to the American mind, and proved that he and Himmler were part of the same machine. We ended with Doenitz.

"The Road to Spandau" led from the German past, and we could pose the question whether it led into the German future. Stindt filmed a local German veterans' rally, and we put a drum beat behind it. As they marched and stood at solemn attention, they looked as they and their older brothers had looked in Leni Reifensthal's film. Harsch's narration ended:

> We do not point a moral. That is not our function. But we do have a point of view, and it is roughly this:
>
> During World War II, the necessities of history dictated that we be allied with the Soviet Union. No one really quarreled with that alliance, but some of us who had been following events inside Russia for the past twenty years were sometimes, perhaps secretly, embarrassed.
>
> This year, or possibly next, through EDC, or if that fails through some other arrangement, we shall become allied with

the German Federal Republic. Once again, the alliance is dictated by history, and no one really quarrels with this. But it might be good taste if we were, even secretly, a little bit embarrassed.

These words made sense because they were written after the film was completed. No less than any drama, this piece of factual presentation had to be plotted and constructed. The difference again was that the plotting and the constructing were done in terms of available material. "The Road to Spandau" was, of course, a tour de force. Having been done, it could not be done again.

This kind of use of available film makes the most satisfying programs. The scheduled program is another matter entirely. I was associated with a program called "Background" for its entire existence, first as managing editor, then as producer, always as writer. The attempt here was to construct, edit, and present film according to all the rules of fictional or dramatic film, using only real materials, real problems, and real persons. Background was unsuccessful—it is no longer on the air.

Of all the individual programs on Background, my own favorite was the story of the Chinese man and wife named Hsieh. She had been a motion-picture actress in prewar China, and active in Chiang Kai-shek's counterpart of the USO; he had been a junior staff officer in Chiang's army. They had met and married while students in the United States. The Immigration Service ordered them deported because they were no longer students. (Neither were thousands more in identical situations who were not deported.)

By the time we started work on the story the two, with their Nationalist records, had been deported to Communist China. We had to make them known through the words of others.

Roger Kennedy, who had come across the story, began by interviewing everyone involved, finding out what each knew and was willing to say. He came back with his notes, and he and I closeted ourselves for a day and made a complete outline of what we wanted and how the program was to look when telecast. This was our "shooting script."

Pearl Buck, a friend of the young couple, told the story. We divided her narration into segments, after each segment picking up a sequence with someone else who had known them, or had acted in their behalf, or had tried and been rebuffed—neighbors; a member of the American Friends Service Committee; the two librarians who had worked with the allegedly subversive husband at the Columbia University Law Library, where he was a bindery clerk; the elderly Philadelphia couple who had been the wife's sponsors when she was in college; the troubled New Jersey Congressman who had written to the Immigration Service and had been told it was all confidential and could not be discussed.

The pieces came into place. We said at the outset that the two Chinese were now in Red China, and at the end that for all we knew they were indeed Communist agents but we could not find proof. The narration ended:

> We do not know that they were innocent. But unless someone can show, and no one has, that there were reasons for deporting the Hsiehs, we cannot escape the uncomfortable conclusion that two gentle and scholarly people were sentenced to Communism because something started the bureaucratic machine to grinding. No one seemed to like what it was doing. But no one could stop it. And no one did.

By itself, in print, this looks like a cold paragraph. But it followed the old lady with tears in her eyes—real tears, not called for in the "shooting script"—reading the wife's letter from Ellis Island: "Although we regret that this has come about, we have no ill-feeling toward the country and her people. We feel that we are living in a time of fear and suspicion. At such a time, hatred often prevails and men often lose their rational power." Or the two co-workers who had taken fresh fruit to them in jail. Pearl Buck: "I used to see them wandering over our landscape like two little figures out of a Chinese screen. They'd walk up from the lake hand in hand, always hand in hand." Or Congressman Frelinghuysen: "There is still the possibility in my own mind at least, that a mistake has been made."

Once, on very short notice, we were told to do a special program on the upcoming British elections. We racked our brains for something original. I happened across a copy of *Punch* that had satirical words, about the accomplishments of one session of Parliament, to be sung to the tune of *This Old House*. We got the necessary permissions, and Cyril Ritchard sang the number. We built around that.

We did a program on the British leaving Suez. Included in the film our cameraman sent back was a silhouette sequence of a bugler blowing the British equivalent of retreat with the flag coming down. We opened with that sequence and went backward.

The cameraman who did our program on the Refugee Relief Act filmed a long sequence in sound with a blind Serbian guitarist playing a lugubrious Slavic melody, with mistakes. He also filmed silent pictures of families wasting away in refugee camps. We played the music behind the silent pictures.

These were acts of writing. Cutting film—sound as well as silent—is an act of writing. Writing is more than putting words together. Writing is also putting ideas together. What happens at the typewriter is only one of many parts of the creative act.

Business Film

The two most important rules about writing business films are: do not be a writer, and do not make movies. In this field you do not—or should not—make movies; you make *tools.* Then too, you seldom write a "story," in the sense of invention; you *find* the story in the true life material.

Nevertheless, you must be an accomplished writer, and you must know a great deal about the technical mechanics of making movies.

Business films—also called commercial pictures and industrial films—are varied in type, but they have one pleasant aspect in common: they are all hits. The producer knows in advance, if his budgeting is competent, that he will take in more money than he spends, without worrying about public acceptance. These films are sponsored; the writing and production costs are ordered and paid for by a business concern or trade association in much the same manner as they would arrange for the preparation of an advertising brochure.

Paradoxically, few of today's business films are blatantly advertising; many of them have nothing at all to do with product promotion. Many are made to improve employee

66

morale, such as *Outside That Envelope,* which demonstrates the benefits under the Connecticut General's group insurance and retirement program. Some are public-service pictures, such as the long-lived *And Then There Were Four* about highway safety, from which Socony-Mobil's only direct profit could come from keeping some of their customers alive—though of course they hoped that gratitude from the public would translate into an institutional benefit. Some are public relations films, such as *The Next Ten,* in which Kaiser Aluminum tells the story of an American business and the men who built it into importance in one short decade. Many product-promotion films are done with scope and indirection: in *Man with a Thousand Hands* International Harvester describes another company's huge construction project in order to show their own crawler tractors —incidentally, the International Harvester name is never once mentioned in Raymond Massey's narration. At present, because many sponsors realize that the public is persuaded more by facts than by pressures, even the forthright product-selling pictures—the airline travelogues and *The K-101 Lint Picker* sort of thing—are likely to be honestly informative and useful to their particular target audience.

These audiences have become surprisingly broad. You yourself may never have seen a business film, but then you may never have been called on the telephone by Trendex or Pulse. The field has been growing rapidly since the mid-'thirties, when 16 mm sound projectors began their steady improvement. Whereas a maximum of some 18,000 theaters book theatrical films in this country, one of the nontheatrical distributors of business films has a mailing list of more than 150,000 groups that regularly show 16 mm pictures. Audiences for 16 mm pictures include 28,000 service clubs, women's clubs, farm organizations, fraternal orders, conventions, libraries, and miscellaneous adult groups; 6,000 industrial plants run films for employees in regular lunch-time showings; 23,000 high schools, 17,000 primary schools, and 2,000 colleges and universities have at least one projector;

15,000 church groups schedule week-night showings, and use many nonreligious, informative pictures; 1,500 small communities are reached in the summer by road-show operators, with 400 persons in the average audience. Certain sponsored films of broad interest may show in some 10,000 movie theaters. Increasingly important is the public-service sustaining time on TV, served by well-organized distributors. A general interest business film like Hilton's *A Hotel Is Born* may be shown as much as three hundred times a year on the approximately four hundred TV stations that regularly use sponsored film to fill out their programing; all the sponsor pays is a few dollars to the booking organization.

In its first five years, *And Then There Were Four* showed to 6,000,000 persons in 50,000 nontheatrical bookings, as well as to 8,600,000 people in 12,000 theaters, 1,300,000 in rural road shows, 3,000,000 in sponsor-arranged meetings, and an undetermined number reached through the 1,000 extra prints sold or loaned, and an undetermined number of watchers of the 715 free showings on TV. The over-all cost per viewer of $00.009 compares well with any other mass medium, and this bought a half-hour's concentrated attention instead of a glance at a page. Although the film is five years old all prints are solidly booked, and it will continue being shown for several more years. I doubt that any of the theatrical features I worked on at Disney, De Rochemont, or MGM has played to a larger audience than this. The point is that business films have become important in the film field and in the national community, and are worth the devoted attention of any writer or film maker.

The word "documentary" means many things to many persons. To the ardent Hollywoodian it means any uninteresting picture in which the actors receive no pay. At the other extreme is the ardently "pure" documentarian, concerned with cinema form and the mystique of "communication," who may be contemptuous toward pictures that admit they have to work for a living. Factual films—the clenched-fist and ain't-it-a-shame polemics, the better-life documentaries, the religious films, the educational and technical and training films, and business films—all have a common blood factor. All are *purpose* pictures. All came into existence because someone wanted someone else to think or feel or decide differently about something. In short, they are "message" pictures.

Surprisingly, to theatrical-film makers, this is all right with audiences—in fact, it is what they want. This does not mean that we are addressing strange and different people—the psychology of viewing is different. The same man who sits in a theater one night and resents a "message" may sit with his wife in a P.T.A. meeting the following night and be equally resentful if the documentary on geriatrics is embellished with extraneous "entertainment." It has been said that no studio ever went bankrupt by underestimating the bad taste of the American public. The factual-film maker feeds a much more deeply rooted characteristic: the universal American desire for self-improvement. Our audiences *want* to be informed.

Borden sells foods, Connecticut General sells insurance, Kaiser Aluminum sells metal, Harvester sells tractors and trucks and farm machines—none of them sells tickets. Consequently they have no interest in "movies" as such, and the business-film maker is wrong if he thinks of his product as movies. The sponsor has a problem or a desire, and he buys from the film maker a tool to help him get what he wants; he would use smoke signals or finger painting if these would work as well for him. The only conceptual kinship between a good business film and a "movie" is the accident of being packaged on long narrow strips of cellulose acetate through which a beam of light shines. The film maker offers tools of persuasion. His product will be better if he always keeps this fact in mind.

The business film is perhaps the most active branch of all film making. The annual production-review issue of the trade magazine *Business Screen* lists several hundred business-film producers, all with quarters and staff, scores of them with complete professional equipment, and several with at least one owned stage. The active production centers are Los Angeles, New York, Chicago, and Detroit, but there are producers in such smaller centers as Knoxville, Minneapolis, and Springfield, Massachusetts. The smaller producers—often two partners with one assistant and an office girl—make three or four pictures a year at budgets usually between $10,000 and $30,000. The colossi of the field—Chicago's Wilding and Detroit's Jam Handy—have hundreds of employees in imposing establishments, and are more accurately called picture "manufacturers" rather than picture "makers." Reasonably typical of the middle group, my own company last year completed seven pictures, ranging in length from eighteen minutes to fifty-five minutes (twenty-seven minutes is the norm), half of them with stage action and synchronized dialogue, the others straight documentary footage with voice-over narration, with budgets ranging from $36,000 through a median of $55,000 to a top of $200,000.

Most of the producers started as cameramen or cutters or production men—seldom writers—usually with a flair for selling or promoting. Many of them make television commercials to help carry the overhead. Most of them do not have much money; they do not need much, because each picture is usually financed by its sponsor in a series of progress payments, the first of which is made in advance on signing the agreement.

As in every area of film making, the writer is a key figure in the making of a successful business film. The salesman is a key figure too, because until a project is sold to a sponsor there is no work for the writer. The requirements for a writer in the business-film field are often surprising; for example, the writer often starts off a project by helping with the sale. The producer usually initiates the contact, does the entertaining, and handles the negotiations. But a business picture is sold only when the sponsor begins to see it shaping into a tool that will solve his problem or fulfill his needs. This often occurs in the initial meetings between the sponsor and the writer. Then the writer begins to be paid rather than to continue to speculate in the hope of getting the writing assignment if the sponsor buys the deal. The sponsor is usually represented by a public relations chief, a sales manager, an advertising executive—seldom an advertising agency—or, in the largest companies, the head of a special motion picture department.

In addition to being a salesman, the writer for business films must be a merchandiser. His assignment is not primarily to entertain—though he must hold interest—but to persuade. In a "product" picture the need for merchandising is obvious. Persuading a large audience to accept an idea, or change an attitude, or comprehend an abstract principle, is merchandising too, although of a higher order. At least 70 per cent of my own "writing" has been done long before I slip the first sheet of paper into a typewriter.

Since good merchandising is built on a thorough knowledge of the material, the writer in this field must be unusually apt at research, with the perceptiveness to recognize useful content and the patience to dig it out. He must read house organs, trade magazines, sales literature, scientific books.

The writer must also interview many persons. This is a peculiar kind of interviewing, by the way, which often involves trickery: the persons are willing enough, but they give you only the obvious information, the facts found in reading weeks earlier. What is needed from them is the sort of sidelit material that, when I was writing for magazines, I called "illustrative anecdotes and significant trivia." One trick is to end the formal interview with gratitude for the wonderful material, and (glance at the watch) "How about a drink?" In the bar, or the coffee shop, or in the man's home, after some casual pleasantries, the conversation can be made to drift back toward the subject of the earlier interview. Then he may say: "Of course, this is no good for your movie, but back in the early days the old man used to test all the experimental bearings in his own car—he drove an old Pope-Hartford with a side crank—and I'll never forget this one time in the dead of winter when . . ." At this point there is only one rule: Do not take a note, or the man may be frightened back to the main currents of American thought.

A writer in this field must know a great deal about the specifics of film production. Obviously he must know costs; for example, he must decide whether he can specify certain shots or must write around them. Even on camera and lighting, he must know whether a certain coverage can be picked up with available lenses; what his interior shots will require in the way of lighting equipment; whether the action in the shot lets him cheat the light by cranking at eight frames; whether he can use window daylight to help on a big color interior if the gaffer uses Macbeths on his booster lights and the cameraman filters out some of the blues. Obviously too, the writer should know something about directing, but a knowledge of editing is more necessary. He must be familiar with the conventional uses of optical effects for screen punctuation. He must also be able to find cutaway shots that will let him play a long scene in short footage without interrupting its continuity with dissolves, and know enough about A-and-B roll printing so that when the negative cutter lacks footage for a dissolve he will switch to a short fade. The writer for theatrical films does not need so much of this mechanical knowledge, since he is writing a series of scenes; a business film is more often a series of shots, of single images laid end to end in an arbitrary progression. There is a parallel with the commercial artist, who needs to know only how to paint, for example, a telephone instrument, whereas the industrial designer of the same telephone must have detailed familiarity with the capabilities of a dozen processes and a hundred machine tools.

Last of all, the writer must be a writer. It is to be hoped

that he has had both articles and fiction printed. In articles he developed his feeling for analysis and logical progression; in stories he developed his sense of plot, his bent for characterization (a tractor can be a "character"), and a thorough professional competence with story construction. He will need all the small tools of the professional writer: the knowledge of how to plant and pay off, how to establish, how to bring out significance by reactions, how to economize words and action, how to maintain suspense (the working of a drill press can be suspenseful), how to curtain a sequence and transition to the next.

The only writer's tool he will not use very much is words, because in the narrated picture, which makes up most of the business film output, the picture should be 90 per cent complete before the words of the narration are considered. This does not mean that the words of the narration are unimportant—everything the audience sees and hears is most important; it means that, to be useful in this specialized field, the writer must add to his skill with words several essential abilities not common to other fields of writing.

The writer should have a clear and orderly mind, with a strong sense of logic and a flair for analysis—including analysis of his craft, because he will do better if he knows why he does what he does—and analysis of his assignments, to determine the basis of what his sponsor needs accomplished. Then too, he needs taste—the good writer's instinctive sense of fitness.

The successful writer must have an active curiosity, and possess what Maugham called the "innocent eye." His eyes should be active: writers naturally tend to formulate their ideas first in terms of words, but here the penalty will be a continuity on the sound track, instead of on the screen in the progression of images. The film writer must think with his eyes.

The writer must have the integrity and confidence in himself to fight for his point of view in the shaping of his film. A frightened or cynical man will shape his film for an audience of one—the sponsor—but the writer with integrity will argue and connive and cajole to make the film effective with its real target audience.

A firsthand knowledge of business and businessmen is also of great value to the writer. When he meets with the sponsor he must, almost by instinct, forget about making a movie and think only about how best to solve the sponsor's problem. The former English major who went directly from college to writing business films will never be at ease in this field; his pictures will not entirely fulfill their real objectives (although they may be effective indeed with a few sponsors whose innocence makes them prey to the "entertaining" film over the effective one). Needless to say, the writer in this field should be emotionally and politically sympathetic to business and businessmen.

Admittedly, this list of abilities and traits describes an ideal. Many writers in the field have fewer of these qualifications but a man will make more effective pictures—and earn more money—if he makes an honest effort to fill his lacks.

To show why these abilities and traits are needed, let us examine the more important stages through which the writer moves, from the beginning when he learns the sponsor's need to the end when a completed film exerts its effect on its target audience.

First, of course, the writer must get the job, usually by persuading a producer of his qualifications.

Then come his first meetings with the sponsor, at which time the writer tries to determine and formulate the sponsor's objective (which should be distilled to a single, short statement) and the target audience.

Research is the next step. With the target audience and objective in his mind, the writer asks himself: "What do they want to know?" and "What do they need to know?" He uncovers everything possible relevant to the subject by reading—all he can, not just a few advertising brochures—and by interviews. This research usually involves travel, to the sponsor's headquarters and to the probable locations where sequences will be shot, because reading about places and people is no substitute for seeing them.

When the writer has his material under control, he develops the merchandising concept on which the whole picture will be built. Whom do we want to think *what?* How will we go about it? *The Story of Menstruation* aimed to drive out fear with fact. *And Then There Were Four* tried to change people's attitudes toward careless driving by showing its effects, not on the victims, but on the innocent persons left behind.

Once the concept has been established, the theme should be expressed in a key phrase. The theme of *Man with a Thousand Hands* was: "With his own two hands a man can do just so much—to do more he must use his mind. The hands of the mind are machines. The man with the machine has a thousand hands—and he and his children a better life."

The next concern is that of the approach. At one end of the range is the direct nuts-and-bolts approach. The natural documentary shows people and things going about their routine business, but with the action edited into a purposeful progression. The *March of Time* format is documentary in its approach, except that past events are reënacted with either "real" people or actors. The semidramatized picture combines narrated documentary with stage-shot sequences. The fully dramatized picture, produced like a theatrical with actors speaking synchronized dialogue in stage sets and enacting a plot, differs from the theatrical mainly in that it contains a frankly stated purpose or message. If the purpose is simply to impart information, the nuts-and-bolts approach is usually best; to make people decide something, the *March of Time* or mixed documentary works well; to achieve an emotional decision or change of attitude, the full theatrical dramatization may be right. By and large, the smaller the average audience unit and the closer their interests to your subject the more straightforward the presentation should be.

At this point, the story frame must be decided upon. I prefer finding the "story" (i. e., the way of telling) in the material rather than inventing a story and superimposing it on the material. The former method usually results in a straightforward presentation, with the author's contribution seemingly limited to selecting the material and arranging it so that the significance becomes apparent.

The formula story has a legitimate use if it is freshened and given for a real purpose. The most important consideration is that a story must be indigenous to the material and the objective.

Pictures that depend upon gimmicks tend to sell the gimmick at the expense of the content, and may entertain an audience without doing much about implanting the sponsor's objective. It is flattering to have a member of an audience say, "You certainly have a wonderful retirement-plan movie here"; it is more pertinent to have him think, after seeing it, "Our retirement plan is better than I realized."

The treatment is simply a description of the proposed picture. It should be done in broad strokes, rather than in detail, so that the sponsor can decide whether the over-all approach to the picture seems right, whether the essential material has been covered, whether the progression seems logical, and whether the proposed film has a good chance of doing what he wants done. The treatment should describe the approach, indicate what facts have been selected from the mass of researched material for inclusion in the picture, arrange these items of content in a logical progression, and impart some feeling of the impression the proposed picture will project to its audience.

After the treatment is completed, the writer and the sponsor have an important conference. Often the eventual shape of the film will emerge only after this meeting. Particularly at this time the writer will receive clarification of certain points that are to be emphasized in the picture as well as useful definitions of policy. Often too, this meeting closes the sale for the producer; earlier he may have had only a script commitment. With the specifics clearly stated in a formal treatment, the producer can prepare a budget, the sponsor can accept it or adjust it, and the production contract can be signed.

In working up the shooting script, the writer faces the difficult problem of deciding how detailed the script should be. Of course, if the approach is a theatrical one, with actors speaking synchronized dialogue, this script will be the final one, with every action and every word carefully indicated. If, on the other hand, the approach is all-location documentary, the final film, shot by shot and word by word, should not be indicated in the shooting script. The writer cannot invent truth; he cannot forecast exactly what the director will see when he arrives on location, with real action and real people. Reality is always more interesting and entertaining and informative than anything invented. Above all, the writer should resist writing any words of narration at this point; reality would have to be restricted or twisted later to fit the set pattern of a narration written earlier.

Movies should be seen more than heard. The eye remembers, the ear forgets; the effectiveness of a movie arises from its ability to implant images, particularly moving ones, in the viewer's visual memory. But the idea or principle of business films usually involves multiple elements; when people must remember several things, they must rely on some sort of pattern. In a movie the continuity is the pattern.

Altogether too many movies have the continuity in words on the sound track, with the images more or less unrelated to each other and glued together by word tricks. If the continuity is in the images on the screen, with one image flowing logically from the one before and leading into the image that follows, the viewer's memory will be visual and more lasting.

Picture content should be simple, inevitable, indigenous. Real simplicity consists not merely in condescending to short words and colloquialisms, but in distilling an idea to its essence—the ultimate seed from which the complex thought can grow. As to inevitability, the writer should be able to put his finger down at any random point of a script and to affirm: "Given these people or things, in this situation and under the established pressures, what is happening here is inevitable—and must be shown." Indigenousness is the materialistic twin of taste. It is a vital check on every aspect of the picture: from determining the fitness of original approach, to selecting fitting visual analogies for the abstracts, to the final editing and narration, and even to the titling, promotion, and distribution of the finished film.

When the shooting script is completed, the meetings held, and the changes made and accepted, the writer has a period of inactivity. Weekly salaries for writers in business films are uncommon; most arrangements are on a "flat deal" basis: the writer agrees to do the job, or stipulated phases of it, for an agreed sum of money. For the total writing job, from initial research through final narration, a fee of $1,000 (plus any travel expense, of course) is fairly common in the low-budget field. The New York producers will pay an established writer $3,000 for a strong-budget job, and fees may go higher for a few writers of substantial reputation on pictures of major importance. There are few royalty or participation deals for writers; the producer's gross is usually established in advance, and the writer's work cannot increase it. Here again, the schedule of four equal payments is common: the first payment (in advance on signing) finances the writer's research and preliminary writing; the second payment (on submission of the treatment) finances his writing of the shooting script; the third payment carries him over the production period, and finances his writing of the narration; the final payment is due on acceptance or recording of the narration. Insist on that word "submission," since "acceptance" is loaded with variables over which the writer's work has no control. The employer (generally the producer, occasionally the sponsor) usually claims the right to cancel at any one of the breaking points, but the writer should be sure of a minimum of two payments, which he needs because of his initial time investment in the research and basic thinking.

Most writers use this production hiatus to start their next job; as in all other types of free-lance work, writers must overlap their assignments to avoid that bankrupting idle time between jobs. A writer might approach the producer to get a production job on his picture, even as a utility man or battery-box carrier if he is new to the field, anything to get some first-hand familiarity with production practicalities. Or he can make a logical pitch for coaching the dialogue he has written, which lets him hang around the director, watch what he does and analyze why. Some writers eventually direct their own scripts.

When the photography is eventually completed, and as soon as the film editor has finished the first rough cut, the writer should be called in for subsequent editorial smoothing, condensing, and polishing. Any factual film should be edited into a good *silent* picture, one that fulfills its objective solely in pictures, before it is ready for narration. If the film medium is used to full advantage, the picture will be reasonably intelligible even to a deaf man.

With the picture 90 per cent completed, at last comes writing the dialogue or narration. At this point, the words are important—enormously important—just as every scrap of sight and sound that goes to the viewer is important.

I begin writing my own narrations by writing the end—the "residual impression" that, if it stays with the audience as they leave the showing (and, it is hoped, for weeks and months after) will achieve the objectives I was employed to fulfill. Ideally, this residual impression is a conclusion to be drawn by the viewer (voluntarily, he thinks), but its trigger is often a carefully distilled theme phrase. This theme phrase will probably be indicated in the opening statement of the narration; it will be touched upon, in a running pattern, several times in the course of the picture.

The most common fault in writing narration is to "call the shot," to describe in words what the viewer is seeing on the screen. There are three cures for this. One, when there is nothing to be said, try not to say anything; let the picture run silently, or with music or sound. Two, instead of depending upon the immediate images or your own cleverness to supply the thought for the words to underlie the shots, go back through your research notes and line up some useful new material content. Three, when the screen image is general, let the words point out something specific; when the image is in close-up, draw a general conclusion or point out a broadened significance. The following questions should be kept in mind. What does the viewer want to know? What does he need to know? What misconceptions should be corrected? What significances should be brought out? And always, what is the residual impression you want to leave?

Narration is constantly fighting the stop watch. In my own tempo of documentary cutting, a shot seldom runs more than five seconds of screen time; even a series of shots that accumulate into one bulk impression will seldom run more than twenty-five or thirty seconds. A writer must write lean prose that sounds casually paced and unhurried. There are many tricks and devices to cheat the watch, but only one principle is involved—distill an overlong thought down to its essence. The ultimate simplicities are always short and immediately intelligible. Once I had five seconds in which to make clear to a children's audience why it was that Jesus had lived in the world's memory when many contemporary prophets had been forgotten. My theological advisers had condensed the material for this spot to twenty pages and felt proud of their accomplishment, but the simple phrase (my wife's) that finally emerged was: "Until Jesus came, people had always been afraid of God." What more need be said?

A truly effective narration seldom reads well on paper. Like a song lyric, it is only part of a whole. If the narration is too coherent by itself, the film probably needs more work. Consequently the narration should be written "to the picture"—physically. I usually get a duplicate workprint of the edited version, have it sound-stripped, and start speaking the narration onto the strip as I watch the progressing picture. For this purpose any one of the magnetic-head 16 mm projectors is suitable if it has a reverse. This projector has the enormous advantage of playing back the equivalent of a finished sound picture. But when the narration plays back, even from an ordinary tape recorder, and the writer listens to it as a stranger, it is amazing how many omissions, misunderstandings, and improvements he will pick up. For what it is worth, by the way, during the time I am supervising a picture through the final edit, and writing the narration, I probably screen the workprint, in the studio and at home at night, between fifty and a hundred times.

When the sponsor has checked the narration script for policy problems and accuracy, the narrator's voice is recorded on tape. The choice of narrator is of fundamental importance; in fact he should have been selected, at least as to type, before the narration was written and its tone set. Because business films must, above all, be believable, the narrator's delivery and projection must be believable. The narrator's voice must have authority and intelligibility, but without being slick and round. At the voice recording, the writer should coach the narrator and be prepared to make necessary cuts and changes. At the interlock session (the first time the several sound tracks are run all together) more adjustments will be needed, some requiring considerable speed and ingenuity. At the dubbing session (when the several tracks are mixed into the balanced composite) the writer should participate in the discussions on how to balance the tracks to get desired effects. Soon thereafter he may attend the first screening of the answer print for the sponsor. Then there are the press *premières* and the meetings with the distributor to help set up the material for the promotional campaign. As I said earlier, in this field it is really total writing.

For the qualified writer, the rewards in this field can be substantial. In addition to the financial returns, the writer will find much greater and more lasting security and stability than he would in the theater or in theatrical films.

The Bespoke Script

The bespoke script, like the bespoke suit of clothes, is ordered in advance to fit the needs of an individual customer. These needs are usually so specialized that the script custom-tailored for one buyer and rejected by him cannot be altered to fit another.

Most of the writing for motion-picture and television series with an established format and set characters is bespoke. Motion pictures chronicling the further adventures of already established characters, like Maisie, Andy Hardy, Mr. Belvedere, Pa and Ma Kettle, Tarzan, and Francis, are profitable when the budgets can be kept down and as long as double billing is common. With the competition of entertainment, where the fee paid by the patron is exposure to the sponsor's advertising, the market for these low-budget theatrical motion pictures has dwindled. But television, largely an advertising medium, is demonstrating its belief that we like what we are used to, and that repetition weakens resistance at the synapses.

Pavlov's dogs learned to associate the ringing of a bell with food. Soon they drooled when the bell rang, whether the food was there or not. So in television the sight of certain

83

entertainers evokes in the consumers' minds the products of certain manufacturers. Television has created a huge market for the hand-tailored or bespoke script.

Hamlet reminds us that the Almighty has fixed His canons 'gainst self-slaughter. For the good of all writers the Writers Guild of America has legislated against speculative writing. Any writer is free to create motion-picture or television material for which there is a wide-open market, where one program's rejection is another program's spectacular. But the man is shortsighted who spends the time and the creative energy necessary to write a script making use of characters and a format owned not by him but by a producer; the writer who does so at the producer's request, with payment contingent upon the producer's approval, is violating both the law of common sense and the rules of the Writers Guild.

Writing to meet the needs of a series should be done at the series' point of origin, certainly after a study of the series by the writer, and probably after conference between the writer and the producer. Before he cuts his dramatic cloth, the writer must know his customer's measurements; he must know whether that customer is willing to place an order with him; there must be an agreement on price. This is bespoke writing. A good Maverick is not an ill-fitting Wyatt Earp lengthened and let out at the shoulders. Robert Young cannot wear Danny Thomas's hand-me-downs. Lassie and Flicka are both quadrupeds, but there the resemblance ceases.

A further argument for thorough preliminary discussion between writer and producer is that each television series has its own taboos, most of them based on the sponsor's business policies. It may be difficult to understand why the phrase "It stinks" is taboo in any script written for a program sponsored by a soap manufacturer, although "It's lousy" is acceptable; compliance with the sponsor's prohibitions, rather than understanding of them, is required of the writer-to-order. Easy to understand, as well as essential to accept, is the absolute rule against drinking scenes or drunken characters, even minor and unsympathetic ones, in any series sponsored by a beer brewer. There is constant pressure from temperance groups to legislate beer advertising off the air. Many sponsors, either through personal conviction or from the standpoint of public relations, will not accept any story in which divorce figures.

Most series have artistic taboos. Lassie may never do anything that an intelligent collie could not or would not do. The Lone Ranger never lies, even to a villain, and never reveals his identity. Officers Friday and Smith never accept even so slight a lagniappe as a ham sandwich from ordinary citizens.

Normal procedure makes either a recognized agent or an established name necessary to the writer who wants to write a bespoke script. Because every unsolicited manuscript from an unknown writer is potentially a bomb, capable of destroying the series, most producers return such volunteer submissions unopened and unread. They may deprive themselves of being the discoverers of genuine writing talents, but they protect themselves against plagiarism suits. The odds against their making an important writing discovery are perhaps a thousand to one, but their chances of being sued for plagiarism are brisk indeed.

The first frail, green shoots of a reputation in any writing field will attract an agent. Established agency representation will enable the writer to receive a personal briefing in the needs of various television series or to learn of them by correspondence. He is then in a position to submit the basic outline of a story, either orally or in skeletonized written form. If the producer is favorably impressed by this indication of the story's essential elements, but wishes to read it in more fully developed form or with changes made in it in accordance with suggestions from him, the writer, without violating the Guild's rule against speculative writing, may furnish him with a two-page outline. For this outline, the producer must pay the writer one hundred dollars, deductible from the writer's first payment if his story is later accepted, but retained by the writer if it is rejected.

Nothing is so rank as the stench of condescension. No writer who feels that a fictional character of exceptional probity and purity, who chooses to wear a mask at all times, is an imbecilic device, should attempt a script for the Lone Ranger. Let him leave the field to those who feel that the Lone Ranger appeals legitimately to children's basic need for escape from the constricting realities of B-4 arithmetic, the daily bath, and the twice-daily tooth brushing, and kindles their admiration for the knightly qualities of kindness to the worthy weak and purposeful anger against injustice.

The television screen is limited in size, and so is the television budget. The length of a television play is as absolute as the length of a sonnet. For a half-hour show, approximately thirty-four pages of continuity must tell a complete story, with a beginning, a middle, and an end, using few and financially feasible sets and a small group of characters. The writer for a series must discipline himself even more rigidly. The bespoke script exacts from its author, in addition to the medium's exactions, the prominent and suitable use of established characters. Loved because they are familiar, they must nonetheless be involved in fresh, new situations.

The writer for an established series earns, hard, every penny he is paid. Though no one thinks he could fly a plane, raise sheep, or tat with no experience, no aptitude, no training, nearly everyone believes he could write if he just took the time to do it. In television, producers, directors, players, sponsors, and account executives are all ready, willing, and believe themselves able to write, or rewrite.

The television writer of bespoke scripts will make some money, and will have the satisfaction of knowing that his audience is in the multi-millions. Against the whetstone of the musts and must-nots of a series, he can sharpen his technique.

Radio

Thirty years ago a high-school friend and I ventured into a Kansas City radio station, armed with fiddle and ukulele, intending to run every other singing team out of business— quite an ambition, for singing teams were then a dime a dozen. Even by the tolerant standards of that time, the results were something less than sensational. Clearly, something new had to be added. So, we wrote a story, a kind of running dialogue, to be interpolated between the songs. It was a radical departure, but if listeners did not like our singing, maybe they would listen to the story. As it turned out, this addition of the written word saved an otherwise mediocre performance. It must have been one of the few times in history when the critics did not report that the "performers rose above their material." In all the years since, I have found no more exciting medium of expression than radio.

More recently, when we in radio watched the rise of the new competitive monster TV, we had some misgivings. We did not know what we could offer in competition to picture *and* sound. We then recalled some of the lessons learned years earlier. After all, we had *always* been dealing with pictures, illusions created in the mind of the listener, whether it be through drama, musical continuity, or commercial. Another old lesson proved even more valuable; only radio offers the great opportunity of establishing *intimate* communication with the listener. Within the remote confines of Hollywood, with its gimmicks and slick production techniques, we had almost forgotten this vital element that had given radio so much universal appeal.

Now, at long last, network radio has begun to establish contact with the audience it has been serving so long.* The crisis seems to have passed, yet we must accept the fact that, so far as the writer is concerned, radio has undergone a drastic change.

Last year, radio time sales were the largest in the history of the medium. Advertisers and network executives have discovered that, in spite of the impact of television, sales of radio receivers have steadily increased and now far outnumber the total sales of TV sets. It is estimated by manufacturers that more than two hundred million radios are in use in the United States. The National Association of Radio and Television Broadcasters estimates more than one hundred and forty million. New radio receivers are outselling TV sets two and one half to one. What is more pertinent and important, it has now been revealed by research surveys that people are listening consistently to radio and apparently have been doing so throughout the past years when programing executives believed the medium to be "dead." Proof that it is very much alive was irrefutable when, last year, officials set up a "big band" live-music program, with the usual interspersed commentary, guest interviews, and news spots, to go out over network stations during morning hours each weekday. In Los Angeles it was necessary for KFI to cancel several soap operas in order to clear

* According to the Radio Advertising Bureau, representing 850 independent stations as well as the four radio networks, the trend back to radio by advertisers is not the result of a sudden awakening, but is a part of a deliberate and intensified campaign of promotion by the RAB—Editor.

time for the big-band program. Within a week the station was so deluged with indignant letters of protest from loyal listeners to the dramatic serials that these were reinstated.

Even so, the demand for dramatic scripts is still limited. The soap operas are usually staff-written, by the network or advertising agency. CBS-Radio in Hollywood originates three dramatic shows: Gunsmoke, Suspense, and the Johnny Dollar five-a-week series. Suspense is occasionally open to free-lance writers; the other two are assigned to contract writers.

A heartening sign in the comedy-variety field has been the return of the Jack Benny Show to CBS-Radio. This is a rerun that uses edited tapes of old shows and does not promise work for the writer at present. But it is important that comedy is considered a necessary part of network programing. Bing Crosby has also returned to his first love: radio; the Amos 'n Andy Music Hall goes on and on, with notable listener and sponsor acceptance. These programs employ a handful of contract comedy writers, the chance of invading the field is limited. Here, as in all writing, it is up to the individual initiative and talents of the writer.

In radio today the over-all budgets are much lower. Yet this fact can work to the advantage of the writer. High quality at low cost is the demand made by modern radio. Thus the creative talents of the writer are more important than ever. Fees are often above established minimums, with newly won rights in ownership of material offering further opportunities for future income.

As of the end of 1957, NBC remains with the Monitor formula on most stations at the expense of dramatic or scripted entertainment. ABC, at this writing, is a music network, employing few writers. In contrast, KHJ and the Don Lee network have recently announced a new program policy, called "Foreground Listening," in which music is held to a minimum with heavy emphasis on talk. This policy is not for improved programing alone. It is argued that a commercial message is bound to have far greater impact when a listener is giving his full attention to the spoken word rather than only half listening to background music from another room. Other stations in the West have successfully adopted this idea, which makes far greater demands in program preparation, with increasing use of writers.

A small but active part of the Hollywood scene is the group known as staff writers. Only CBS-owned KNX and the Columbia Pacific network employ such writers under a WGA staff contract. They write for radio alone, in contrast to their Eastern counterparts, who double between radio and television. Most continuity writers in Hollywood serve in the dual role of writer-producer. Again this is a step forward in bringing the creative talents of the writer into the production picture. By the nature of their work, staff writers are divided into two categories: continuity and news. Staff continuity is a field well worth the young writer's attention. It demands broad talents not always required of the free-lance or contract writer. The continuity writer must be a craftsman in all areas of programing. A dramatic writer is rarely called upon for the quip or punch line so necessary to the comedy writer, whereas the comedy writer lives in a world of laugh tracks. By contrast, a staff continuity writer is constantly faced with assignments in all fields, except the news. He may be trying his hand at comedy one day, drama the next, audience participation the next, plus an occasional documentary, commercial, or variety show. Thus, although he faces the danger of being labeled a jack-of-all-trades, he nevertheless has an opportunity of gaining at first hand a broad working knowledge of radio production around the clock. He sits in department conferences, and has a hand in the creation of new ideas and new programs. He works closely with both production and sales departments, and follows his written product through from its inception to the broadcast.

A place for the beginning writer is indicated in the WGA staff contract, with provisions for advancement. This is well worth the student writer's attention. On the debit side, staff contracts have a long way to go in the matter of continuing rights in ownership of material, and staff minimums are lower than those enjoyed by the self-employed free-lance writer. The continuity staff writer has a reasonable amount of security in his job, regional and network commercial fees, paid vacations, pensions, insurance, and other advantages enjoyed by the company employee.

The staff news writer works exclusively on reporting, evaluating, and writing the news. Throughout the period of "readjustment" in radio, when other programs went by the boards, news not only held its own but gained an even more commanding position—more news programs, more news writers.

One important fact must be mentioned to the young writer who aspires to the network radio news field: rarely if ever does a network news bureau hire a novice, no matter how skilled he may be as a writer, unless he has had thorough training in the news medium. Although an experienced newsman can be trained quickly to the requirements of radio broadcasting, a writer cannot easily acquire the skill of news writing. Because of this fact, nearly all network news writers are recruited from the staffs of large city newspapers. That is where the opportunities for practical experience lie, from the copy desk up. News reporting is a career in itself, and one must know his profession well before becoming a part of this group of specialists.

Again a warning must be given to the writer who seeks news experience on a small station. Usually this entails little more than taking the news from the teletype. The teletype is only an end product, and provides no dependable stepping stone toward a network news assignment.

The ambitious staff news writer will find opportunities for moving forward. The next step may be that of the combination writer, editor, newscaster. Beyond that is the commentator, the man who has established himself as an authority of high merit and experience in world affairs.

Still another opening for the radio writer is often overlooked: the advertising agency. These agencies have a tremendous need for good copy writers for radio and TV commercials. A copy writer often ranks along with the staff artist and the account executive in his organization. After all, without effective sales copy, the finest show with top ratings is of little value to the sponsor. The agencies also originate most of the dramatic serials that fill much of the daytime programing.

Anyone who is adept at turning a phrase and creating slogans, who gets excited about the idea of selling words, should consider this important field of writing. And it *is* writing in every sense of the word. Salaries for beginners are low, starting at $60 or $70 a week, but established writers in the Hollywood area earn as much as $12,000 a year. Occasionally the chief copy writer in a large agency is also the vice-president, if that is any encouragement.

Since few commercials are now written in the offices of radio stations or networks, it is logical that the place to begin is in the agency itself. Practical education should begin in a small agency, preferably outside the big production centers where most of the recruiting is done.

The dramatic narrative show, one effective answer to radio's low-budget problem, can be easily tailored to five, ten, or fifteen minutes, depending upon the sponsor's need. Program costs are limited to the salaries of writer and narrator. Certainly the importance of the writer is obvious, in his ability to bring scenes and characters to life through the spoken word alone. Good examples of the narrative show are Marvin Miller's Behind the Story and the Jack Moyles' Point of Law. The once-popular dramatic program Don't You Believe It has now been revised to the narrative format, and the others will follow.

The documentary program also continues to hold a unique place in radio. More often than not it is a one-time-only show designed for a specific purpose—to commemorate an important event, launch a drive, or perhaps expose a social problem. Because of the prestige-building potential, a sponsor will often assign an unusually high budget to the one-time documentary, making possible the use of cast, orchestra, sound effects. Here is a welcome opportunity for the writer, but he is faced with a problem beyond that of the ordinary dramatic script. He is dealing not with fiction but with facts—often, cold and seemingly uninteresting facts. Production tricks, music, multiple use of voices, once the mainstay of the documentary writer, are not enough now. The writer must set out first to find some facet of characterization or narrative that will intrigue and entertain. If he fails in this, the documentary will also fail, victim of the intense competition for listeners that prevails in broadcasting today. Again the field is limited, but there will always be a place in radio for the skilled documentary writer.

Although all this may not hold out a very encouraging prospect for writers in contemporary radio, there is a definite current trend that may well provide a very strong market within the next year or so. Radio time sales for the current period have reached a record high level: radio advertisers are now beginning to buy time segments instead of the multiple short commercial spots. Consequently there will be an increasing demand for programing content. The writers who can originate dramatic material to fit the low-budget production requirements, and at the same time provide new dimensions of sound for the old reliable and still most popular medium of radio, will come into their own.

Meanwhile, the best training ground for the new radio writer is still a small station. He may not have the opportunity of writing much at first, but here he can mentally prepare himself for any phase of broadcasting and can develop an attitude for accepting the continuing day-to-day pressures. He can thus acquire a solid foundation of experience on which to build a future in writing for radio, television, or screen.

Writing Contests

The new writer receives occasional encouragement from script contests. Some of these contests are announced simply as an aid to the writer. Others are announced as aids to freedom, Americanism, safety, international understanding, education, intergroup harmony, and other causes.

Because some contests are not so beneficial to the writer as they may seem, and because others are better than they seem, it is well to have a good look at contest rules.

The Queens County Bar Association in New York conducted a contest for college and university students, for the best half-hour dramatic television scripts dealing with "American principles and the political philosophy embraced in the Constitution of the United States of America, the Declaration of Independence, and in our traditional concept of democratic government." So far, splendid.

The prizes were modest—first prize $150, second prize $100, third prize $50. No objection can be raised to this, because such sums are welcome to most students.

However, in order to enter this contest, the young writer was required to sign a release: "In view of the fact that the Queens County Bar Association is sponsoring a television script writing contest and has offered prizes and other considerations to entrants in that contest, I . . . hereby transfer to the Queens County Bar Association all of my right, title and interest in and to my script, including the right to procure a copyright thereof in the United States and any other country, upon the understanding that my name will be mentioned, as author, whenever my script is produced or published."

It should be noted that the Queens County Bar Association thereby became the owner, in entirety, of every script submitted, whether or not it won a prize. The association had the right to copyright the script, and it owned all television rights, radio rights, stage rights, film rights, publication rights, recording rights, adaptation rights—internationally.

Now an ineffective, incompetent script may be worth nothing. But how much is a good script worth?

Before we try to answer that question, it should be made clear that the aim of the Queens County Bar Association in this contest in no way required the acquisition of *all* rights. When asked why such insistence, a representative of the association's Committee on American Principles explained that it wanted to make scripts available to high schools and colleges for use by their dramatic groups, and wanted to be able to authorize broadcasts "for educational purposes." This could have been accomplished very simply, by means of an entry blank licensing the distribution of winning scripts to schools and colleges for specific, local, nonprofit uses. The writer could meanwhile have retained film rights, publication rights, and other potentially valuable rights of no apparent concern to the association.

A more satisfactory arrangement has been made by the University of Maryland in its script contest, open to students of any college or university. The 1955 prize for the best half-hour script was $500. The contest rules clearly stated: "The University of Maryland will reserve rights to the first production of the award winning script only . . . Subsequent production rights become the property of the author. Rights to other entries remain with the authors."

As with the Queens County Bar Association contest, promotion of the Maryland contest was directed to the television-radio departments of universities. Many of these departments felt obliged to point out to students that an entrant in the Queens County contest relinquished ownership of his script whereas an entrant in the Maryland contest retained ownership, giving up only "first production" rights, and only if he won a prize.

The two contests mentioned above awarded comparatively modest sums. A contest launched by the Fund for the Republic, open to anyone, offered many prizes, including two of $5,000, two of $2,500, and others of $1,500 and $750. The purpose was "to advance the aims of the American people as they are expressed in the Declaration of Independence and the Constitution." But the rules stated: "All entries become the property of the Fund for the Republic upon submission. Winning entries will remain the property of the Fund. It is the intention of the Fund to release the rights to non-winning entries upon written request of the authors."

Why should entrants have to ask in writing to have ownership restored to them, with only the assurance that the fund had the "intention" of doing so? Why should winning scripts "remain the property of the Fund"? Was this a wise provision? Was it in any way necessary to the work of advancing the aims of the American people as expressed in the Constitution? * Clearly it was not. The effect was merely to discourage the interest of professional writers. The fund did revise its contest rules, but too late to have much effect on contest submissions.

Concurrently with the Fund for the Republic contest, Talent Associates, writers' representatives and packagers

---

* The Constitution includes a pertinent clause, on which our copyright legislation is based: "The Congress shall have the power . . . to promote the progress of science and useful arts, by securing for limited times to authors and inventors the exclusive right to their respective writings and discoveries."

of Armstrong Circle Theater, Justice, and other series, sponsored a contest for half-hour plays by college or university students. First prize was $1,000, second prize $500, third prize $250. The prizes were substantially smaller than those offered by the fund for the Republic. But note the contest rules.

All scripts remained the property of their writers. Talent Associates acquired, *for a limited period,* an exclusive option to produce the winning script on television. If the script was produced in this period, the writer would receive a minimum of $1,000 including the prize. Thus the contest sponsor acquired limited, specific rights. Other rights belonged to the writer.

When a television script is unsuccessful on the air, its subsidiary rights may have little or no value. On the other hand, if it is successful, subsidiary rights may be far more valuable than the original television rights. Motion-picture rights in successful television scripts have sold for as much as $60,000—occasionally more. Certain television plays have become Broadway plays, earning many thousands in extra revenue. Publication rights, foreign rights, radio rights, recording rights may all yield revenue. That is why it is impossible to answer the question: "How much is a good script worth?"

Decades ago a playwright often had to surrender ownership of his play to a producer to get a Broadway production. The Dramatist Guild did away with this practice. In the early days of film and radio the outright sale of literary property was common. In the current minimum basic agreements of the Writers Guild of America in film, radio, and television, one of the most important features is the separation of rights. Separate negotiation is held for such rights as first broadcast rights, reuse rights, theatrical film rights, television film rights, and many other rights.

Writers know that writing is hard work. Most writers have a limited number of years of top production. Their security may depend upon being able to develop literary properties that will continue to yield an income through various uses. Consequently writers have learned to protest and resist any arrangements that relinquish literary property outright. Such arrangements, too often, merely bury scripts in the files of organizations unable to use them or to get them used. Sponsors, foundations, and associations that insist on "all rights" should realize that such a demand now has the effect of sending the writer elsewhere.

In examining contest rules, the writer should ask:

Does the writer retain ownership of his script, or does he surrender it?

What rights does the contest sponsor acquire through payment of the prize? Is the prize a reasonable payment for the rights acquired?

If the contest leads to use of the script for a commercial feature film or sponsored network telecast or similar use, will the applicable Writers Guild of America minimum basic agreement apply?

If winning scripts are to be published in book form and sold through bookstores, who will receive the royalties?

The Writers Guild of America, East and West, is always ready to help organizations in the framing of contest rules, with the aim of making these rules acceptable and attractive to the writer—an important factor to the success of any script contest.

LOLA GOELET YOAKEM

The Business of Writing

Dr. Samuel Johnson once said with sagacity that to write for any reason other than for money is ridiculous.

Samuel Goldwyn, who holds a similar belief regarding the production of motion pictures, paid a million dollars for the screen rights to *Guys and Dolls*, plus an additional amount on such rights when gross receipts from the production exceed ten millions. According to Goldwyn, the story is like the foundation of a building. "Who's in a picture is secondary: a big cast means nothing if the film hasn't a solid foundation: but to make a picture today is not enough —the whole world must know about it." Letting the whole world know is the purpose of exploitation, publicity, and promotion. Big-budget movies can be box-office failures without the right kind of exploitation; conversely, some low-budget productions have made big profits because of properly planned promotion. Goldwyn has respect for the story and for exploitation because he has respect for profit. If writers are to be successful they should achieve similar attitudes, because writing is just as much a business as movie or TV production.

There is probably no realm of endeavor more fraught

99

with varying and conflicting opinions than the story business. There is no exact formula for a hit. Movie production today is in the hands of independent producers. The tinsel era of big studio organizations is largely a thing of the past. A modern producer acquires a literary property that presumably appeals to him, and then he gets a commitment from a star; with these in hand, he obtains his financing. Thereafter, with efficient promotion for his product, he may get his money back and even make a profit.

Television has become a market for motion pictures: the old ones, of course, as well as the new ones being made for closed-circuit television. TV is also a source of story supply for theatrical films. But most important to the writer is the vast and continuing market that television programing provides. The writer must know his way around the business if he is to succeed in selling his wares and making a profit from them.

Profit is money, and, in the manuscript marketplace, where the commercial businesses of television, motion pictures, and radio buy the foundations for the entertainment they manufacture, nothing succeeds like money. The money a writer receives for his script represents economic security to him, of course, but the sale also gives him an increasingly marketable commodity in the form of credit. All business depends upon credit for its operation; a commercial writer's business success is his *writing* credits—his stockpile of by-lines, proof of his professional standing. Only a thorough understanding of the business end of writing can give a writer the constant protection he needs to assure receipt of this most valuable stock in trade. He must understand every clause of the contracts he signs, and must make sure he is guaranteed in writing the number, size, and shape of his credits, not only on the finished product, but in all subsequent advertising and promotion that may be done in connection with it.

The Writers Guild has done an outstanding job in bringing about recognition of the writer and his place of importance in the fields of radio, television, and motion pictures. The Guild continues to secure advantages for the writer, not only in minimum basic working agreements with producers, but also in the protection of credits.

Now we are beginning to observe a degree of exploitation for the writer and the script. Honor for the commercial author has been a long time in the making. No one knows why. It may be that the earliest writers were obscured because most people were unable to read and therefore to enjoy the written word. Again, perhaps the fabled nonentity of the author made him a prize target for those unscrupulous persons who sought to turn his knowledge and work to their own selfish advantage. If Stephen Foster had not been so dedicated a song writer, and therefore willing to give away all rights to his work in order to get it published, the world might never have known of his talents. Unfortunately, selfish motives still remain to plague the naïve and unsuspecting writer who may be bilked of his credits and profits in many cynical and cunning ways. Although the entertainment field today is more secure for the writer than it ever was before, it still offers little safety for ivory-tower writers.

Publicity will help protect an author's work. It has many other advantages as well, including the establishment of the writer's name. Some writers do not want publicity; some contracts even forbid an author's seeking or accepting publicity for himself or for his script. Yet we live in a world of advertising. People believe in advertising—it is a vital part of every business, including the writing business. A successful writer must understand business administration. The writer who is also a businessman does not waste time and energy in casual talk. He puts it in writing and gets it in writing; he makes sure he understands the fine print, both in his conversations and in his contracts.

Modern commercial writing is a business more than it is an art. It is a business in which the writer is production, management, and sales. He must constantly deal with persons in other businesses; although they do not need to know anything about his business, except whether his product pleases them, he must know a great deal about them and their product and business policies.

A knowledge of business methods will aid a writer in the protection of his work. Present copyright laws still do not afford him complete insurance against loss. A man can invent a machine made of anything except words and music, and the federal government will afford him stringent protection of his rights. The abstractions of literature and music are, however, still vulnerable under the existing laws— "coincidence" may cover a multitude of plagiaristic sins if the writer cannot prove his prior right. Proper and prompt registration of scripts is important. A dated journal of work progression, extra carbon copies and notes, orderly filing systems, and complete card indexes on manuscript submissions—all are valuable necessities of a writer's business. A writer's businesslike approach to handling and marketing of his product is prerequisite to his success. A writer must know how to manage his business as well as his thoughts and time. Many guild writers have managed so well that they are not wholly dependent upon script sales for livelihood. Some have become producer-writers because of their successful business knowledge.

A writer wishing to enter the commercial fields of television, motion pictures, and radio should understand his objectives. Every beginning writer has something to say which, he thinks, is of vital importance. Soon he discovers that he is writing what an editor will buy, or what an agent believes can be sold, or what he has been assigned to write —none of which may bear any relation to what the writer *wants* to write. Even the more free-ranging novelist must write what a publisher wants to print. Poets are probably the only writers who can enjoy freedom of written expression, because, unfortunately for the advancement of culture, they do not have to worry much about sales potential or audience ratings. Writers of commercial entertainment must have realistic objectives. There is no place here for the purveyor of precise syntax as such. No matter how you phrase your work, remember that a reader or a listener will assimilate your words according to the restrictions peculiar to his own ability to interpret, his knowledge of word meanings, his individual experience factors, and his total personality pattern.

A free-lance writer's first task is to get his script read. The first reading may be done by a junior reader, who works in his spare time on a per-script pay basis. If the script gets past him, it then goes to a senior reader, thence to the head of the story department, and thereafter to producers or editors of various programs for which the material is suitable. All this routine takes a great deal of time, and time is money. Therefore most scripts produced on television or in the movies are usually written by a small group of professionals who can reach production heads with story ideas, submit brief story lines, and possibly secure an assignment to write the script. Again, because entertainment is a business, a movie producer who is restricted to a predetermined budget may prefer to buy a stage play, even though it has been a failure in legitimate production or has not even been produced on the stage, and have it adapted by a writer whose credits indicate he may turn it into a money-making vehicle.

The financing of motion-picture production has, for the most part, always been secured through bank loans. In a tight money market, however, many firms have been augmenting cash reserves by public stock issues as well as by straight interest loans from their exhibiting circuit owners. Many independent producers obtain their operating capital from one of several sources: their own personal funds; private straight interest loans from individuals; private participation and percentage loans; major studio corporations, who may be interested only in financing and distributing; bank money, when the loans can be backed by sufficient collateral. Television production is financed in much the same manner except that, unlike current movie-

making practices, there are more large production corporations than independent producers turning out programing on film which they finance entirely as well as produce
and distribute. There are also some examples in which
TV networks finance independent production on a partic-
ipating basis. A few Broadway stage productions have been
financed in exchange for future TV rights. The book of *Look
Homeward, Angel* is owned by Paramount Pictures; the stage
play, based upon the novel, is a box-office hit, and, consequently, will be sold for motion-picture use. For this reason
the buyer of these dramatic rights will be obliged also to
make a deal with Paramount.

It is interesting to observe the results of ingenuity at work
when a tight money situation brings about the necessity that
mothers invention. Kenya Productions, Inc., with permanent
studios in Nairobi and Rumuruti, East Africa, is such a result.
This firm is a recently set up subsidiary of Gross-Krasne,
Inc., a pioneer American independent producer of television
films. Many film makers trek to Africa for location shooting,
but Gross-Krasne is the first to undertake a permanent
business location there. When the American money market
became tight, financing for the productions in the United
States was difficult to arrange. After the company had made
plans for an adventure series to be filmed in Africa, President Krasne made a trip to Nairobi with a friend who is
in the banking business. Through this connection Krasne
met the officials of Barclay's Bank in Nairobi. The bank had
a problem, because prestige and wealth in Kenya are established by the number of goats a man owns. The bank
wanted to convince the Kenyans that it is better to put
their money in the bank than in goats. They had made
a business film with this message, but they did not
have enough theaters in which to exhibit it. Krasne suggested that a short entertainment film from his firm's
inventory be run in conjunction with the bank's film, both
to be shown from projectors mounted on Gross-Krasne trucks.
Seconds later the natural course of events led directly to

Barclay's financing Gross-Krasne productions. Such financing was worked out in this manner: a principal loan source for film makers in New York is Bankers Trust Company, which in this instance issued letters of credit to Gross-Krasne. Through these letters of credit Bankers Trust assumes the risk of the loans made by Barclay's to the producing firm. The Nairobi bank earns 6 per cent on such loans, and Bankers Trust receives 2 per cent for underwriting the risk. Gross-Krasne has therefore been able to secure enough financing to set up its East African studios and to proceed with production there, as well as to make use of a part of these funds to continue its production in the United States. The subsidiary, Kenya Productions, was organized to avoid a time-quota restriction imposed on non-British TV films—not more than 14 per cent of British television programing may be filled by foreign productions, thus bringing about competitive price wars among American producers and their distributors vying for this limited British market. By means of a subsidiary in British-controlled Kenya, TV films using British technicians and actors qualify as British-made; instead of a top two thousand dollars that one thirty-minute episode may return on an American-made film, a minimum return of six thousand dollars may now be expected. There is also a production economy on African labor cost amounting to an average of two thousand dollars per segment less than United States costs for a similar filming.

Good business sense has long indicated that the writer of screenplays should have more connection with and influence in the promotion, planning, and selling campaigns of the finished motion picture, but writers have always been kept so much in the background that audiences may often assume that the actors ad-lib the screenplay.

No other industry excludes the originators and creators of its product from all knowledge of marketing and sales. That this has been the custom in the making of movies may be one of the reasons contributing to the dearth of good profit-making films. It may well be that the economy achieved in the *Marty* production and its resulting impressive profit came about because of the close working association of writer, director, producer, and distributor. More recently, the producer of *Peyton Place* consulted the screen writer in advance discussions of exploitation being planned for the movie; the screenplay was thereafter so plotted as to provide provocative scenes that lent themselves to publicity angles deemed advisable for reaching various audience groups.

No one can tell a writer exactly how he can solve his unique problems of script selling, which is in most respects like a game of chess. No two chess games will ever be identical, but experience teaches the player what move to make and how to know the right time to make it. No writer or chess player can win every time.

The writing of commercial entertainment is a serious and a dignified business. A writer assumes a very real obligation to humanity when he enters this field, because millions are influenced and indirectly educated through the media of television, movies, and radio. It is the business of today's writers to guide and educate as intelligently as possible within the confines of audience acceptance and media limitations, and to create a better written product for a better world.

The Hollywood Market

Countless unpublished writers come to Hollywood hoping to break into movies, television, or radio. It is a sad but nevertheless inescapable and routine fact that disillusionment and rejection will face most of them.

In these days of disc jockeys and news reporters, radio has little need for new dramatic writers, although this market seems to be opening up.

Movies are bigger and wider and better than ever, but not necessarily for the budding author. When a studio pays a quarter of a million dollars for a best-selling novel or a smash Broadway stage hit, it will not entrust the adaptation of such a high-priced property to a newcomer. A veteran writer with top credits will get the assignment. There is, however, a definite indication that the increasingly high prices being asked by publishers and legitimate play producers for motion picture rights will probably force movie producers to revert to the original screenplay market. Some book publishers are said to be asking as much as $500,000 for screen rights even before publication. The original screenplay was much in demand for many years until the vogue for so-called pretested properties took over. Some movie studios are now looking for such material, but with little enthusiasm or hope

107

of finding any potential money-makers in unpublished form. Because producers cannot afford to gamble on untried and unproved material, they want something that is pretested by an approving mass audience: such as *The Young Lions, A Farewell to Arms, Peyton Place, Bonjour Tristesse, Witness for the Prosecution, No Time for Sergeants, Desire under the Elms*—or they buy the film rights to a live TV play.

In the two years after the purchase of Paddy Chayevsky's prize-winning TV play *Marty*, the movie studios bought more than thirty such TV plays as bases for future films, including two other Chayevsky plays, *The Catered Affair* and *Bachelor Party; Patterns* and *The Rack* by Rod Sterling; *Crime in the Streets, Dino,* and *Twelve Angry Men* by Reginald Rose; *Ransom* (telecast as *Fearful Decision*) by Cyril Hume and Richard Maibaum; *Fastest Gun Alive* (telecast as *The Last Notch*) by Frank Gilroy; *Bail Out at 43,000 Feet* by Paul Monash; *The Midnight Story* (telecast as *The Eyes of Father Tomasino*) by Edwin Blum; *Zero Hour* (telecast as *Flight into Danger*) by Arthur Hailey; *The Young Stranger* by Robert Dozier; and *Man on Fire* by Malvin Wald and Jack Jacobs.

The sale of motion-picture rights to *Man on Fire*, in which I was involved, was an example of a star looking for a story. Bing Crosby saw Tom Ewell in *Man on Fire* on TV, and told movie producer Sol C. Siegel about it. Siegel in turn arranged for the MGM story department to negotiate for the purchase of the property. This example points up how often the element of luck can influence a sale of literary material.

The problems of breaking into live television emanating from the west coast are similar to those in New York. Some of the biggest shows from Hollywood are Playhouse 90 and Desilu Playhouse. Material submitted to these shows, particularly by an agent, will be read.

The field in which Hollywood clearly dominates is television films. Here, more often than not, doors remain open, and many hopefuls are making their first sales.

Television films have eclipsed the live shows in broadcast time, both network and locally. It is, of course, true that most of the work is done on assignment by experienced television writers, many with a hundred or more produced shows to their credit. These writers came to television with backgrounds as produced playwrights, published novelists, and short-story writers, or as writers with many years' experience in radio or motion pictures. Thus, it is only natural that a television producer, faced with the enormous task of turning out as many as fifty-two films a year, should rely primarily on these veteran writers.

This situation applies to nearly all the variety comedy, situation comedy, and episodic shows.

A variety comedy show is one in which a comedian appears every week in a variety of unrelated comedy sketches or blackouts, rather than in one complete story. The George Gobel–Eddie Fisher and the Perry Como shows are prime examples of this type of program. Since a very definite and peculiar comedy style is required, the producers use experienced and skilled writers who fully understand the Gobel, Fisher, and Como techniques. The Jackie Gleason Show was a live, hour-long variety comedy show until it was decided to use one set of characters, the Honeymooners, for a filmed half-hour program. The Honeymooners was a perfect example of a situation comedy show. Every week the same characters were involved in a complete story. Perhaps the most famous show in this category has been I Love Lucy. Others include You'll Never Get Rich (the Phil Silvers show), Make Room for Daddy (with Danny Thomas), Life of Riley, December Bride, Father Knows Best, Mr. Adams and Eve, Burns and Allen, Ozzie and Harriet, People's Choice, Oh! Susanna (with Gale Storm), Mama, Life with Father, and The Real McCoys.

Like the situation comedy, the episodic drama has one or more principal characters in a new story every week. Examples, in mystery, crime, and adventure, are Dragnet, The Line-up, Wyatt Earp, Gunsmoke, Public Defender, Foreign

Intrigue, Meet McGraw, Richard Diamond, Have Gun, Will Travel, The Restless Gun, Wells Fargo, Cheyenne, Maverick, Sugarfoot, Jim Bowie, Wire Service, The Thin Man, Highway Patrol, and Whirlybirds.

The producers of situation comedy and the episodics have also learned that it is more efficient and economical in the long run to hire only experienced writers, who are quick to understand the needs and limitations of their individual shows. They rarely consider outside material.

Where, then, is there opportunity for the ambitious new writer to earn the vital credits that attest his experience? The answer is in the anthology.

Anthology shows are those with no continuing dramatic characters, but rather a series of separate and distinct dramatic shows. Examples are: The Loretta Young Show, Jane Wyman's Fireside Theater, Alfred Hitchcock Presents, Schlitz Playhouse of Stars, General Electric Theater, Millionaire, Telephone Time, Science Fiction Theater, Navy Log, The Silent Service, West Point, and Zane Grey Theater.

These programs obtain scripts in one of three ways:

1. An experienced writer *tells* the producer an idea. If the producer likes the idea, he has the writer prepare a story outline, for which the writer is to be paid. If the outline is acceptable, the writer is then hired to proceed with the teleplay.

2. The writer submits either a published story or a written story outline. The producer buys it and may have the original author—or another writer—prepare the teleplay.

3. The writer submits a complete, original teleplay. All producers are desperately searching for scripts that are ready to shoot, from which a budget can be made, that can be sent to the sponsor for final approval.

This last approach, then, is the best—and possibly the only —way for a new writer to break into television.

The inexperienced writer is well advised to take a high-school or university-extension course in writing specifically for TV, preferably with a teacher who is a professional TV writer or who is acquainted with agents and producers. Such teachers are anxious to recommend the work of talented students to agents, who often come to them in search of new scripts.

While teaching at the University of Southern California I was impressed by the writing ability of a young man, and sent him to a small literary agency. Within five months two of this student's scripts were sold to the anthology series Chevron Hall of Stars.

Similarly, a young real estate salesman, discovered by an agent at Hollywood High School's evening classes, sold scripts to Cameo Theatre, Matinee Theater, and U. S. Steel Hour. Film rights to the U. S. Steel script, incidentally, were later sold to Paramount Pictures.

When writing an agent, describe your script and ask if he would care to read it. In your letter include your background: education, any courses in writing, names of teachers, and also a list of any published material to your credit—books, magazine stories or articles, newspaper articles—or any experience in radio or in playwriting.

The chances of selling to Hollywood TV producers without an agent are very slim. The producers prefer to deal directly with responsible agents, who will weed out the dull, the bad, and the impossible scripts before making submissions. A list of literary agents may be obtained from Writers Guild offices in Hollywood.

Perhaps the best possible preparation for selling a program is to pick out a market and study it carefully for the taboos, the style, the type of material used.

Then sit down and write. If the material is really good, sooner or later you will find a market for it.

The New York Market

If television has done nothing else, it has certainly trans-
formed us into a nation of critics. Day after day, and night
after night, untold millions sit with their eyes glued to their
sets and watch with interest, fascination, exhilaration, and
even boredom. It would be contrary to human nature to
expect the entertainment simply to flash upon the screen
without very decided and articulate reactions from the home
audience. And so, many conversations today are concerned
not so much with the price of meat, the danger of war, and
the weather as with the state of Arthur Godfrey's health,
the performance of George Gobel, and the gentle earthiness
of Eva Marie Saint in her latest effort on an hour dramatic
show. In short, everyone has an opinion, and has learned to
express it forcibly and directly.

Television is even turning us into a nation of creators also.
There will always be some brave souls who will not stop at
criticism—they will want to go on to higher fields. Why not
write a show and collect some of the money that the networks and the sponsors pay for the words that come between
the commercials? Somebody has to do it, and no one can
be blamed for trying.

If some amateur sits down and does write a television play, has he any chance of selling it? The answer is in the affirmative—but it is not a very loud yes. Television, like the stage, screen, radio, and publishing, is generally a professional medium. Most successful television writers have come up through the ranks, as have the successful dramatists, screen writers, and novelists. They have achieved success by observing the same rules that have always applied to serious professional writers.

As a matter of fact, most television writers have come into the medium from the other fields, particularly from the theater. These have not necessarily been successful playwrights with Broadway hits to their credit, but they have had some experience in writing plays. This is still the best groundwork for the television writer and the one that pays off. Writing for radio and screen also provides a good background for the newer medium.

The fledgling television writer should have some kind of writing experience, some knowledge of the technique, and a great deal of patience and determination.

The largest market for scripts is still New York, although Hollywood is rapidly assuming greater importance. Many of the dramatic shows produced in Hollywood still buy their material in New York, particularly for "live" shows. It is felt that since live television began in the East the New York writers are better acquainted with the technique of this medium and have had more experience in turning it out effectively. The filmed shows are much more Hollywood's province.

Both NBC and CBS maintain story departments where material is submitted and bought for the various network shows. CBS will not ordinarily read unsolicited manuscripts unless the author has a list of credits or is recommended personally by someone in authority. NBC does not follow this policy so rigidly. It has one show, Matinee Theater, which puts on five one-hour dramatic shows a week and whose staff will consider material that is sent in from unknown sources. Recently Matinee Theater devoted a week to plays by authors who had never before had a television show produced; the results were gratifying. This show is an exception, however, and maintains this policy only because its demand for stories is so great. Both networks are interested in the work of college students who are taking courses in television writing for credit, and the recommendation of a professor or teacher may carry considerable weight.

Any writer submitting a script should know in advance whether he is writing a half-hour or an hour script and for what show he is aiming. Further, he must conform to all the rigorous technical demands of this exacting field. There cannot be too many characters or too many sets, and the more tightly the script is written the better its chance of selling.

Most established television writers are represented by agents, and most shows prefer dealing with authors who are so represented. Reputable agents can save clients and buyers much valuable time by carefully examining material, making suggestions as to just what stories are needed in the market, and acting generally as trouble shooters. An unknown writer, trying to crash this highly competitive market, is in a much better position if he sends his script to an agent before he even considers letting a network, a packager, or an advertising agency look at it. The prospective buyer knows that a good agent will not submit a script unless it has some merit. On the other hand, agents will not read unsolicited manuscripts unless they have knowledge of the author's background and experience. Some agents will give editorial advice and criticism on a script, and charge a small reading fee for this service; if the script is sold, the fee is returned.

Although television devours material at an alarming rate, it is a field for professionals and not for enthusiastic amateurs. The competition is tough, but the financial rewards are increasing—more and more writers are devoting their entire time to television instead of using it as a somewhat precarious sideline.

About ten one-hour, live, sponsored dramatic shows are put on the air every week by the networks. According to the basic contract between the Writers Guild of America and the networks, the minimum payment for a one-hour dramatic show is $1,100 for an original play and $815 for an adaptation, although most shows pay considerably higher. This is for only one use of the material; all the basic rights belong to the author. Recently a trend has been to sell TV plays to motion pictures. At least forty plays have been sold to pictures in the past year or so, and television is regarded as the most important showcase for stories that will eventually become movies.

Television writing is now becoming respectable and dignified, as shown by the fact that CBS is now putting television writers under contract, as the movie studios formerly did and seldom bother to do now. The writer is guaranteed a certain amount of money yearly, and in return can do any extra work he wishes. Again, these contracts are awarded to the writers of dramatic shows of an hour or longer.

The moneyed aristocracy of television is undoubtedly the select group of comedy writers. A first-class writer of situation comedy, sketches, or gags can command almost any price. This ruling class has come up the hard way from vaudeville, musical comedy, radio, and even from the comic books. A neophyte in this field has hardly a chance, although NBC is making a thorough and determined search for new comedy writers.

Then there are half-hour live shows, half-hour film shows, documentaries filmed and live—all of which require written scripts. Many of these shows are in the hands of packagers, who either use their own writers or seek out new talent. The filmed shows can be much more remunerative for the writer than the live. Each time a film is shown, either on the network or in syndication, the author has to be paid again. These residuals, the rate of compensation of which has been carefully worked out by the Writers Guild, have recently become important as a source of income for writers. Variety shows, interviews, and even weather reports and news broadcasts need writers.

One of the outstanding features of any kind of television writing, from the preparation of a five-minute news broadcast to the enormous amount of time and effort that goes into a ninety-minute color spectacular, is the constant pressure to which everyone is subjected. A certain amount of rewriting is always necessary because of the split-second time schedule that all shows observe; there are always cuts to be made or new material inserted, stars to be placated, and directors rescued from the psychopathic ward. The writer very often finds himself in the midst of this general insanity. His is no ivory-tower occupation. He is expected to be present at rehearsals—and should be if he wants his work to emerge in anything like the state in which it was conceived.

The New York television market is a rather inbred circle, and one that is difficult for a newcomer to crash. If he manages to get an agent's attention with his script, then the agent must submit it to the network story department. If the story department approves, it goes to the script editor of the show for which it is destined. From the editor it goes to the producer. Finally, the script must be approved by the advertising agency that represents the sponsor. The writer who emerges successfully from these ordeals must be talented, resourceful, and ready for any eventuality.

Sometimes a script is subjected to cuts and changes that seem to destroy the force and point of everything the author has tried to say. Compromises must be made all along the line, and freedom of expression is limited. The taboos are so many and so far-reaching that it is impossible to list them all. Television is an advertising medium whose main purpose is to sell goods. The sponsor must avoid offending anyone in his audience. In spite of all the strictures, no television writer anywhere can help but thrill to the fact that what he writes will be seen by millions who will perhaps be a little moved or entertained by his work. This great, uncountable audience cannot be reached by any other means. Aside from the monetary consideration, this is the real fascination of television writing—the size of the audience.

Abbreviations of Trade Associations and Organizations

ABC   Audit Bureau of Circulation (Advertising Media)
ACE   American Cinema Editors
AFM   American Federation of Musicians
AFTRA American Federation of Television and Radio Artists
ALA   Authors League of America
AMPAS Academy of Motion Picture Arts and Sciences
ANTA   American National Theatre Association
ASC   American Society of Cameramen
ASCAP American Society of Composers, Authors, and Publishers
ATAS   Academy of Television Arts and Sciences
ATFA   American Television Film Association
ATFD   Association of Television Film Distributors
BMI   Broadcast Music, Inc.
FCC   Federal Communications Commission
IATSE   International Alliance of Theatrical Stage Employees
IBEW   International Brotherhood of Electrical Workers
MOA   Music Operators of America
MPAA   Motion Picture Association of America
MPIC   Motion Picture Industry Council
MPPA   Motion Picture Producers Association
NARTB National Association of Radio and Television Broadcasters
NSTP   National Society of Television Producers
NTFC   National Television Film Council
RAB   Radio Advertising Bureau

Abbreviations

SAG	Screen Actors Guild
SDG	Screen Directors Guild
SMPAD	Society of Motion Picture Art Designers
SMPTE	Society of Motion Picture and Television Engineers
SPA	Songwriters Protective Association
SPG	Screen Producers Guild
TBA	Television Bureau of Advertising
WGA	Writers Guild of America (E, East; W, West)

Glossary

ADAPTATION   Transforming of written material from one form to another.

ANIMATION   Photographing of inanimate objects to depict action.

BALOP   Projection of still photographs or signs through slide machine called balopticon.

BG   Background.

BIG CLOSE-UP (BCU)   Closest camera range.

BIT   Smallest speaking part.

BIZ   *See* BUSINESS.

BLACKOUT   *See GO TO BLACK.*

BOOM   Crane holding camera for mobile shots.

BRIDGE   Music or sound used for scene transition.

BUSINESS (BIZ)   Visual action to establish characterization and advance plot delineation.

CLIMAX   Highest point of dramatic action immediately preceding resolution.

CLOSE SHOT   Position halfway between medium and close-up.

CLOSE-UP (CU)   Camera shot at close range.

CONFLICT   Opposing factors in action or characterization.

CREDITS   By-lines in finished film product.

CRISIS   Obligatory scene resulting from proper plot delineation.

CROSS-FADE   Fading out one image and fading in another.

CUE-IN   Shooting-script term, used by director, meaning to start action.

Glossary

CUT (CUT TO) Fast switch from one camera to another to give increased pace to the progression of scenes. In radio, indicates finish. In TV and radio, refers to part of script that may be deleted for timing purposes. *See also* DISSOLVE.

CUTAWAY A suspense-building flash of secondary plot action related to principal action.

CUT IN (INSERT) Usually a close-up of object inserted to explain a segment of action.

CUT TO *See* CUT.

CU *See* CLOSE-UP.

DISSOLVE Slower than CUT; gradual fade out of one scene and fade in of another. *See also* LAP DISSOLVE.

DOLLY BACK (DB) (PULL BACK) Move camera away from subject.

DOLLY IN (DI) Move camera toward subject.

DRUM A barrel-like cylinder over which titles and credits are rolled in front of camera.

ECHO Sound transmitted through electronic device to give hollow reverberation effect.

ESTABLISHING SHOT A scene that sets the mood and introduces a character.

EYE PICTURE An idea or impression transmitted to the audience by specific props and business.

EXPOSITION Opening scenes that set the stage for plot advancement.

FADE IN (FI) Gradual process of image appearance on screen; a blending of one scene into another.

FADE OUT (FO) Reverse of FADE IN.

FILTER Any device used to give special tonal effects to sounds and voices.

FI *See* FADE IN.

FILM CLIP Stock film scenes screen-projected within a live TV production.

FLIP CARD A TV title card that is turned by hand or mechanically. *See also* BALOP.

FO *See* FADE OUT.

FOOTAGE Length of film on reel.

FORMAT Unchanging structure and pattern of TV show or script.

FRAME One complete picture on film. Thirty frames constitute one second of motion picture.

FULL SHOT Camera shot to include all characters in scene.

GO TO BLACK (BLACKOUT) TV script direction for screen to appear suddenly black; used for dramatic effect.

IN CLEAR (IN COLD)   Music or sound cut in at normal volume and without any other accompanying sounds or voices.

IN UNDER AND HOLD   Bring sound or music in under action and retain to cue out.

INSERT   *See* CUT IN.

INTERCUT   Camera alternates between two sets or two separate bits of action or two characters on the same set.

IRIS IN   Changing focal length of lens to effect close-up from close shot.

LAP DISSOLVE   Same as DISSOLVE, except fade in overlaps fade out.

LIP SYNC   Synchronization of sound track with filmed movement of lips and mouth or action.

LONG SHOT (LS)   Full, over-all shot of complete set including full-length shot of characters.

MATTE or MASKING SHOT   Film expression indicating part of a set to be built and part is painted on glass and shot.

MEDIUM CLOSE-UP (MCU)   A shot including only the upper part of the actors.

MEDIUM LONG SHOT (MLS) (MEDIUM SHOT)   Halfway between a long shot and a close shot.

MIRROR SHOT   A shot of a reflection in a mirror.

MOVING SHOT (RUNNING SHOT; TRUCKING SHOT)   A shot in which the camera moves along with subject.

OPEN END   In TV or radio, the time left at open and close for commercials.

OFF STAGE (OFF SCENE) (OS)   In TV, out of camera range.

OUT-OF-FOCUS DISSOLVE   *See* TRANSITION SHOT.

OVER FRAME (OVER SHOT)   Script direction indicating that sound is heard but source of sound is not seen.

PAN   Slow swing of camera for panoramic view.

PAN DOWN   Reverse of PAN UP.

PAN TO   Camera direction to follow movement across a set or to give panoramic view of set and then focus on character.

PAN UP   Camera focuses low on subject, then moves slowly up. *See also* PAN DOWN.

POINT-OF-VIEW SHOT   *See* REVERSE ANGLE.

POP   Musical fanfare or flourish for finish.

PROGRESSION   Action development in plot toward the CLIMAX, tying loose ends together.

PROCESS SHOT (STOCK SHOT)   Filmed scenes made previously on a process stage, clips from which are projected on a rear screen behind action being photographed.

PULL BACK   *See* DOLLY BACK.

RESIDUAL   The writer's ownership rights in his material, reverting to him after a stipulated period during which he has leased it.

REVERSE ANGLE (POINT-OF-VIEW SHOT)   A shot on a second camera opposite the main camera; or a shot made by turning camera and focusing it exactly opposite to its original position.

RUNNING SHOT   *See* MOVING SHOT.

SEGUE   Musical bridge from one theme to another without an obvious break.

SNEAK   Start sound at low volume and fade in.

SPLIT-SCREEN SHOT   Images from two cameras filmed or transmitted in one frame simultaneously.

STING   Music flash or fanfare brought up sharply to accent a scene or climax of a scene.

STOCK SHOT   *See* PROCESS SHOT.

SUPERIMPOSE (SUPERIMP)   Overlap two images in one frame.

THREE SHOT   A group of three subjects.

TIGHT TWO SHOT   Heads of two subjects.

TIME LAPSE   A visual method to indicate passage of time.

TRANSITION   Scene changes advancing the story without production interruption.

TRANSITION FOCUS (OUT-OF-FOCUS DISSOLVE)   Blur image of one scene and gradually clear the succeeding one.

TRUCKING SHOT   *See* MOVING SHOT.

UNDER   Retain while voice or sound is heard.

VOICE WAY OFF   Voice off stage.

WHIP   Sudden swing of camera to blur image.

WIPE   Quick replacement of one scene for another in transition.

X   Direction for actor to cross the set.

ZOOM (ZOOMAR)   Quick change of focal length in lens from long shot to close shot; also a Zoomar lens.